SPRING BREAK

A True Story of Hope And Determination

TMSC Publishing Co.™
Upper Saddle River, NJ USA

By: STEVEN BENVENISTI, ESQ.

TMSC PUBLISHING CO. ™
Upper Saddle River, NJ USA
TMSC PUBLISHING CO. ™ is a registered
trademark and may not be used by any third
party in an unauthorized manner.

ISBN-10: 1469903644
EAN-13: 9781469903644
Library of Congress Control Number: 2012902901
CreateSpace Independent Publishing Platform
North Charleston, South Carolina

Steven Benvenisti
Attorney at Law

This is a work based on real events. Although extensive efforts have been made to accurately recreate events, locales, and conversations from memories, a diary, extensive notes and conversations with others, names and dialogue may have been altered to protect the privacy of the individuals involved.

Although this book demonstrates that one can fully overcome the impact of a severe traumatic brain injury, please keep in mind that this book is not a substitute for the professional advice of physicians, PhDs, and/or therapists. Every brain, emotional and/or orthopedic injury is different and must be dealt with according to the specific needs of the individual and family.

This book merely provides one individual's story to shed light on the serious nature of driving under the influence. It is my hope that the words within will provide inspiration for people everywhere.

DEDICATION

For my family: Dawn, Robert, and Laura.
You are by far the biggest and best accomplishment of my life.

PART ONE

THE CRASH

I didn't start MADD to deal with alcohol. I started MADD to deal with the issue of drunk driving.

~ Candy Lightner, MADD Founder

CHAPTER ONE

EARLY GRADUATION GIFT

"Imagine the worst thing that could happen to you, something so horrific death is a welcome alternative."

I looked out over a crowd of more than 500 teenagers lounging on gym bleachers as I spoke. Someone coughed and a few fidgeted.

I cleared my throat, unsure if my words were getting through to them. One or two seemed to be considering my suggestion, but most were giving me that blank, disinterested stare reserved for lecturing adults.

Who could blame them? I'd been lectured more times than I cared to count during my high school days to learn about the virtues of such things as why I shouldn't, "Become a father before I was old enough to vote," or why drugs and alcohol were, "very, very bad." Those adults always droned on in preachy, self-righteous voices, with an underlying message that equated to, "You're young and don't know anything." I'm sure the students thought I was about to give them a similar boring lecture.

Instead of the mall hair and parachute pants of my high school days, my audience had nose rings and tattoos. Though the style had changed, the attitude was still the same. I was well aware that I was nothing more than a get-out-of-class-free card to most of them. I hoped to give them much more than that by the end of the hour.

"Hey, what's the only kind of good lawyer?" jeered a particularly tough looking kid with messy surfer hair.

"That will be enough, Curtis," admonished the principal.

As a personal injury attorney, I get my share of ambulance-chaser jokes, but the truth is I'm very proud of what I do. I make a difference.

1

Every person who comes to me is in need of help. They're almost always alone, with no one to fight for their rights, or offer the support they desperately need; and they've all lost something dear—something that until recently they most likely took for granted, like a healthy back, use of their legs, or total mental capacity. They have many questions. They want answers to help restore a little of what they used to have.

While I can't bring back their previously healthy condition, I can help them get justice; money damages to bring them a quality of life that's been taken away from them, cover their medical bills, and live the most comfortable life possible under their new set of circumstances. It was just such a case that led me to stand in front of this motley group of high schoolers. The case touched me like no other. It was so gruesome, so unthinkably devastating, that I often got chills just thinking about it. In fact, it gave me nightmares. And so I'd made a promise. I promised that if I won, I would spend the rest of my life educating the public on the cause of this case—drunk driving.

The unusual heat of early spring in New Jersey was stifling in the small gym. My audience was talking in a growing whisper, despite the disapproving looks from teachers. I had to get to the story quickly, or lose them for good.

"Today, I'm going to reveal a secret so precious, that it not only saves lives, it guarantees success."

"Can it make me a million dollars?" shouted Curtis.

I looked directly at my heckler and smiled. "It could, if you want it to. The really cool thing about this secret is that it can work for anyone, anywhere, any time. But to understand how it works, you'll need to hear about the most significant case of my career. While a few of the names have been changed, this story is absolutely, one hundred percent true."

The looks on the faces of my audience were skeptical, but the gym was noticeably quieter.

"This case took place right about this time of year. It was spring break. Twenty-one year-old Ben was an all-American college student. He had everything going for him. He was an athlete, president of the honor society, and had a great job that came with his having a private on campus apartment. He was also vice-president of a popular fraternity and had a pretty girlfriend. He was very close to his family—two

2

sisters, a brother, mother, and father. It seemed everyone loved Ben, and he loved life.

"As a way to reward himself for all his achievements and an early graduation gift, Ben decided to take one last college spring break trip down to Daytona Beach, Florida. Little did he know, that trip would alter the course of his life forever..."

Chapter Two

THE NIGHTMARE BEGINS

Daytona Beach, Florida, March 20th

"Make way for MTVs newest star." Jack bowed down to Ben, as his fraternity sponsor entered the hotel room.

"Is it true?" asked Ace. "Did you really get on TV?"

There'd been rumors circling all afternoon that Ben judged some kind of bikini contest on MTV. There were 50 brothers in Theta Chi Fraternity and it seemed like every one of them was crammed in the room to hear their charismatic friend's story. He was a confident guy, muscular with thick dark hair and a perfect tan, the kind of person producers ate up.

"I might have done a little something this afternoon," grinned Ben. He walked to the fridge and grabbed a Coke.

"Details, dude," coached Jack as the brothers juggled for better positions to hear *Ben's Epic MTV Adventure.*

"I don't know," said Ben, taking his time. "I might need a little incentive." He fingered one of Ace's finely tailored Italian shirts hanging in the open closet. While Ace was known for his excellent taste in clothing, there was one shirt Ben and most of the other fraternity brothers had always wanted to wear.

"Oh no, not my shirt!" Ace shook his head. "No one wears this shirt but me."

Ben shrugged. "Then I guess I'll have to go back to my hotel in order to get something to wear for tonight. I'll probably be late getting back and have to meet you at a noisy bar, where no one will hear me even if I shout the story."

The brothers looked from Ben to Ace.

"Come on, give him the shirt," encouraged one of the guys.

"Yeah, it's only a shirt," appealed another.

The whole room started chanting, "Shirt, shirt, shirt."

Ben shot Ace a good-natured, gottcha smile.

Ace shook his head. "Fine, I'll give him the shirt."

Ben's grin widened. He reached for the white V-neck with brown stripes, but Ace grabbed his arm. "This shirt better come back looking and smelling the same," he whispered.

Ben nodded, "Thanks Ace, I'll take good care of it. I won't even eat or drink in it."

"You better not even perspire," Ace said with a smile.

Ben drew an imaginary X over his heart. "I promise."

Ace held two fingers to his eyes and then pointed at Ben, "I'll be watching you."

"Relax," chuckled Ben slipping into the soft fabric. He admired himself in the mirror, noting the way it made his tan stand out. "It's in good hands."

Pleased with the exchange, the fraternity brothers started a new chant, "Store-ee, store-ee."

"My fans await," Ben said hopping onto the bed to address the guys. "My spring break is complete. Being on MTV was totally awesome! There were hot chicks everywhere in some of the smallest bikinis you could ever imagine."

"So how'd you get so lucky?" asked one of the guys.

"Guess they just liked my look."

"Yeah right," someone at the back of the room said as a pillow sailed towards Ben.

He ducked just in time.

"Watch my shirt," yelled Ace.

Everyone laughed and more pillows flew through the air.

"Gimme a break guys," shouted Ben as he dodged the incoming missiles and headed for the door. "Let's hit the bars."

The guys partied through the night, moving from club to club. They were used to not having a central party location. Because they didn't have a fraternity house back home, they were constantly moving from one brother's rented abode to another's. It had never stood in the way of a good time. But the indoor parties during the long New Jersey winter had taken its toll on them. The ocean air and warm wind was just what they needed. The pretty girls didn't hurt either. It was paradise on earth.

At any other time, Ben might have regretted his promise not to eat or drink in the borrowed shirt, but he was having so much fun that it didn't matter. There were plenty of interesting people to talk to and beautiful women to dance with.

Little by little the group splintered off as they found dates or headed to other bars, until only Jake, Patrick, and Ben remained.

Around midnight, two muscle-bound jocks started picking on a smaller guy.

"You lookin' at my girl?" taunted the larger of the two.

"N-no," said the small guy, taking a step back. "I was just trying to get through."

"I think he's trying to get somethin' over on you," said the other jock, coming up behind the little guy.

The little guy, holding up his hands, said, "Look, I don't want any trouble."

"I don't like the looks of this," said Ben.

"Come on," Jake reminded him, "you're wearing Ace's shirt."

"His shirt will be fine," Ben said distractedly. If there was one thing he couldn't stand, it was bullies. He had once been just like the little guy, until he joined the football team and started lifting weights. He might not be as big as those two apes, but he could surely help the little guy even the odds.

"Is there a problem over here?" Ben asked, placing himself directly between the jocks and the little guy.

"What if there is?" sneered the bigger thug.

"I was just thinking, it's much too nice a night for getting my knuckles all bloody."

The big guy snorted. "I don't have a problem with you. Step aside."

Ben held his ground. "But I have a problem with you. You see, I don't like it when I see innocent people getting picked on. So I'm going to have to stop you."

"You and what army?" laughed the other thug.

Ben pointed in the general direction of his two friends and the large group of people behind them. "It'd be a shame if we had to take you out to the parking lot and teach you a lesson."

The big guy shook his head and stepped back. "It's not worth it."

His friend lingered. "You're just going to back down?"

"I said it's not worth it!" barked the big guy, walking away.

"Thanks," said the smaller guy, extending his arm.

Ben shook his hand. "Don't mention it."

"Another minute and I might have been toast." He frowned and looked at Ben, "You might have been toast too."

"Forget about it. No one's going to the hospital tonight."

"All the same, thanks, again," said the little guy, disappearing into the crowd.

"You bet," Ben smiled as he returned to his friends.

"I don't believe it," Jake joked. "Ace's shirt's all right."

Ben rolled his eyes, "I'm doing fine too, thanks for asking."

"How'd you get those two guys to back off?" asked Jake.

"I told them we and all those guys behind us would take them out."

Patrick twisted to see who was behind them. "But we don't know those guys."

Ben raised a brow, "But they didn't know that."

"Oh great guru, teach me your ways," laughed Patrick.

Ben frowned. He felt jittery all over and began to shake. He hadn't been in a fight since the fourth grade. If his ploy hadn't worked, those creeps would probably be kicking his butt right now. The whole thing made him feel sick.

"Hey, you all right?" asked Patrick.

Ben gave a half-hearted smile. "Yeah, I'm fine. Only I think I'm done with death-defying stunts for the night. Let's get outta here."

"What's this I hear about your hundred ways to meet a woman?" Jake asked as they began to walk.

"It must work, how else did you get on MTV?" agreed Patrick.

"My brothers, you've come to the right place. I have a technique for every day of the week and every hour of the day."

"Give us an example," said Patrick.

"Oh you want an example? Well how about the foreigner?"

"How does that work?" asked Jake.

"Simple. I pick out a pretty young lady, put on a very thick accent, and tell her I'm from Greenland and just arrived in the country to find my future wife!"

"And women actually fall for that?" asked Patrick.

"Well, no, not usually, but it is a technique," laughed Ben.

"Come on man, you gotta give us something that works," begged Patrick.

"Ok, ok, but I think it's best if I demonstrate," said Ben heading towards the boardwalk. The others quickly settled up their tab and followed.

"There's always the direct approach," explained Ben. "Find yourself a group of girls and pick out the prettiest one."

"Like those girls over there," Jake gestured with his head.

"Perfect," said Ben. "Watch and learn."

He walked straight up to the prettiest one.

"You're absolutely beautiful. Can I give you a kiss?" asked Ben.

The girl with long blond hair blushed and giggled. "Ok."

Ben planted a sweet kiss on her cheek. "Thank you."

Patrick and Jake watched in amazement as Ben made his way back over to them.

"Dude, she said you could kiss her and you didn't even go for the lips!" howled Patrick.

"Being a gentleman pays off," laughed Ben. "It makes them want you even more."

As if by magic, the girl Ben had just kissed walked up and handed him a slip of paper. "I thought you might want my number, in case you get bored."

Ben grinned. "Thanks…I didn't catch your name."

"Candy," she smiled.

"Thanks, Candy, I just might do that." Ben waved as she returned to her friends.

"Dude, that was absolutely amazing," hooted Patrick.

"Yes," agreed Jake. "Show us more."

"Ok, ok," laughed Ben. "This next one is high drama. I call it the sympathy approach."

A beautiful redhead was backing her convertible out of a parking space just as Ben approached her. He cupped his hand and hit her empty trunk. A loud thud sounded through the night air.

"I've been hit! I've been hit!" yelled Ben falling to the ground.

"Oh no, oh my G-d!" cried the horrified redhead jumping out of her car. "Did I hurt you?" she asked leaning over him and gently touching his shoulder.

"I see an angel," he said sitting up.

The redhead sat back on her heels. "You're all right?" she asked narrowing her eyes.

"I will be if you give me a hug," Ben said smoothly as she helped him to his feet.

She was so relieved that she hadn't hit him that she gave him a hug before driving away.

"Dude, you are so lucky she didn't deck you," marveled Patrick as the trio headed toward their hotel.

"It's a tricky one," joked Ben following his friends down the street. "But stick with me gentlemen. When you learn from the master, you'll never go wrong."

"We hear you, we hear you," laughed the fraternity brothers, crossing the street to their hotel.

"Sure, walk away, those who are afraid..."

BANG!

Patrick and Jake turned just in time to see a late model car traveling the wrong way down the street with its headlights out crash right into Ben. Everything went into slow motion as the two helplessly watched Ben slam onto the hood. His legs were crushed on impact. His torso violently struck the windshield, followed by a sickening smack as his head exploded through the glass. Dagger-sharp shards showered down as the sweet smell of radiator fluid filled the air and Ben's lifeless body tumbled like a ragdoll across Ocean Avenue. He came to rest face down, in a gushing pool of blood.

Patrick and Jake raced the 70 feet to Ben as if in a dream. People were screaming; traffic came to a stop.

"Help us! Somebody please!" screamed Patrick looking up into the gawking faces of the growing crowd.

"Call 911!" yelled Jake.

A couple hurried to the nearest pay phone.

Ben's body lied still and face down in the street. A growing puddle of blood began to collect on the dark asphalt below his face and to the left of his head. His lower legs were visibly disfigured, with his right leg, "Pointing in six different directions," per one eyewitness.

"Why bother?" said a half-drunk spring breaker in Bermuda shorts. "The dude's a goner."

"No! Don't say that!" choked Patrick, lunging at the guy. "You don't get to say that."

Jake pulled him back. "That won't help Ben."

"We're nursing students, let us through!" shouted a female voice.

Two dark-haired girls made their way through the crowd. They knelt by Ben and took his pulse. "He's still alive!" the taller one screamed. "Give us your shirts. We need to stop the bleeding."

Several guys quickly ripped off their T-shirts and handed them over.

Sirens could be heard in the distance as the nursing students worked to save Ben's life.

Down the road, the driver of the vehicle still sat in the twisted scrap of metal, dazed and very, very drunk.

"Johnnie, Johnnie, wake up," slurred his girlfriend, Julie, "the cops are gonna be here any second."

"Oh, my head," moaned Johnnie.

"I know baby, but we gotta switch places. Another DUI and I'll never see you again."

He mumbled incoherently and obediently flopped across the seat, letting her crawl behind the wheel.

"Hey, hey, I see that!" shouted a spring breaker, who'd come to check on the occupants of the vehicle. "They're trying to switch places!"

A group of on-lookers rushed over for a better look.

"No, this is the way we've been," Julie argued. She put a hand up to her right temple. Her head was spinning terribly and she felt like she might throw up.

"We should get them out and put them back in the right seats," suggested one of the on-lookers.

"Thanks, I'll take it from here," said a police officer patting the witness on the back.

The homicide team had been dispatched to the scene. While Ben was still alive, chances were it would soon be a murder investigation and Daytona Beach Police liked to be thorough.

CHAPTER THREE

MIDNIGHT CALLER

The phone rang well after midnight. Doris' heart lurched. She knew it was something terrible, even before her husband, Hank, answered. "Yes, I see," was all Hank said.

She looked at him, her eyes wide with fear. There was only one possible explanation; her other three children were all safe in bed. "Is it Ben?"

Though alarm bells went off in Hank's head, he tried to remain calm. He turned slightly away from his wife as she tugged on his arm so that he could hear what was being said. Mental images of trauma scenes and ERs filled his head as the police detective told Hank that Ben had been rushed to Halifax Medical Center.

"How serious is it?" Hank asked when the detective finished.

The hair on the back of Doris' neck stood up. It had to be really bad for anyone to call at this hour. Ben wasn't the type to get in trouble. She tugged her husband's arm again. "Is he…" the words hung in the air. She couldn't bring herself to ask if her third child was dead.

"We'll be waiting," said Hank placing the receiver back in its cradle.

Doris tried again to get the words out. "Ben, is he…all right?"

"No," said Hank. "There's been an accident. A drunk driver hit Ben. They want us to keep the line open so the doctor can call us in a little bit."

Doris swallowed. "Is it bad?"

"I don't know. But he said he was rushed by ambulance to the hospital. If the doctor wants to speak to us in the middle of the night, it's probably not good."

"Oh no," cried Doris as tears began to flow down her face. Great sobs shook her body until she thought she might pass out. She felt sick and dizzy all at once.

Hank gently put his arm around her shoulders. "You've got to relax and stay calm. We don't know anything yet," he said rubbing her back. Truth be told, he felt like he might go into shock at any moment too, but he knew he had to remain emotionally detached or risk escalating Doris and his other children into a panic.

"It's going to be all right," he reassured Doris. "We have to stay strong and in the present so we know what to do when they call back." He handed her a tissue as she sat up.

"This can't be happening. This is a living nightmare."

Hank took her by the shoulders. "We don't know anything yet. You need to stay positive."

She took a deep breath, but couldn't stop the tears.

"Can you at least try?" he coaxed.

She nodded. "I'll go wake the kids."

Within minutes, 25-year-old Debbie, 24-year-old Bruce, and 20-year-old Michelle were all assembled in the family's kitchen.

"Did they say when they'd call?" asked Bruce.

"No, just to keep the line open," replied Hank.

The family sat in silence staring at the beige phone on the wall. Its cord hung in a tangled mess of curlicues from years of winding and unwinding as Ben and his siblings had stretched it to the limits, crushing it in one door or other in the attempt for a little privacy.

The plastic clock above the sink ticked off the minutes. During the day it was barely audible, yet at this hour it sounded like a freight train, echoing through the room at a deafening decibel.

Michelle yawned. "It's probably nothing. You know how Ben is, always exaggerating."

Her mother frowned. "Ben didn't call. It was the police."

Her dark eyes snapped into focus. "Dad, is that true? The police?"

He nodded.

"Oh my G-d, Mom, it's going to be bad, really bad," she said hugging Doris.

"Now we don't know that," said Hank rubbing her shoulder. "It's best in these situations to think positively." He looked at the others, "Worrying won't do us a bit of good."

They nodded and fell back into silence, as the deafening tick of the clock filled the room once more.

Every minute that passed seemed like an eternity to Doris. Hank's words might be good advice for the kids, but that was her baby out there. How could she not worry?

Bruce and Michelle's heads were almost on the table when the phone rang. Debbie jumped. Doris' and Hank's eyes locked for the briefest of seconds before he picked up the receiver. He gave his family a reassuring smile.

"Hello?"

"Yes, this is Dr. Rogers from Halifax Medical's trauma center. I'm calling to update you."

"Yes?" Hank said pressing the phone tight against his ear.

Dr. Rogers spoke with the practiced, unemotional tone of a seasoned trauma professional. Over the years he'd learned that it was best to speak slowly in plain English. Most of his patients and their families were incapable of understanding much more.

"Both the patient's legs have been crushed below the knees. The bones have been shattered and some pieces are missing. Much of his frontal flesh has been torn away from his lower left leg, and he's also missing a sizable portion of skin and muscle from his lower right leg and his clavicle is broken."

"I see," said Hank silently praying he'd heard the worst of it.

"He's also lost a lot of blood and is receiving a transfusion as we speak."

"Ok," said Hank mindful to keep his voice steady as four pair of eyes watched him intently from around the kitchen table.

"Unfortunately, this is not the worst of it. He is in the deepest coma possible. He has been unresponsive to any stimuli, painful or otherwise."

"I'm sorry, I don't understand what that means," said Hank, turning to ignore Doris' pleading eyes.

"When someone is in a coma, we measure the severity with something called the Glasgow Coma Scale. It ranges from the deepest level of coma, which is a three, all the way up to a fifteen, or full consciousness.

This patient is a three. He doesn't respond physically to pain stimuli, nor does it register on his life support monitors. We'll perform a CT Scan shortly to determine the extent of his brain damage."

"I see," said Hank pacing the well-worn tile. It seemed strange that the doctor kept referring to Ben as "the patient." He didn't like the negativity coming from this man, who held Ben's life in his hands. "Doctor, what are my son's chances of survival?"

Doris closed her eyes and put her face into her hands as the others broke into tears.

Hank pulled the phone cord tight, working his way into the other room so that he could hear the doctor over the sobs and sniffling.

"The news isn't good," said Dr. Rogers. "The team that's been working on him doesn't think he'll make it more than a few hours. If you want to say your good-byes, you need to get over here immediately."

Hank inhaled deeply. "I understand."

"Before you go, I need to ask, have you thought about donating his organs?"

The breath caught in Hank's throat. This couldn't be happening. He thought he was going to get a call about a few stitches, maybe some broken bones, not asked about arrangements in case of death. It was all a bad nightmare. He'd wake up soon and tell Doris about the horrible dream. He waited for a full minute and time stood still with him.

The phone line crackled, "Sir? Are you still there?"

He didn't trust this person who wouldn't call Ben by name.

"Just do everything you can to keep him alive. Treat him like a patient that you are expecting will survive."

"I understand," said Dr. Rogers as the line went dead.

CHAPTER FOUR

REALITY SETS IN

Later that same day, Ben's parents arrived at Halifax Medical Center. They anxiously took the elevator to the intensive care unit. Hank lightly squeezed Doris' hand as they rode the six floors up. Her eyes were red and puffy. It felt as if a permanent waterworks station had been installed in her head. She wiped her lashes with the same tattered piece of Kleenex she'd been carrying since that morning. As silly as it sounded, part of her felt like she could control things by only using one, as if the more she used, the worse things might get.

"We need to be strong now and stay positive," Hank reminded her.

Her skin was pale and there were growing dark circles under her eyes, but she gave him a small smile. "Always."

He gently kissed her before the bell rang, announcing their floor. "We will get through this."

The door opened and she sighed. "We always do."

"You must be Ben's parents," a tanned nurse with bleach-streaked hair greeted them.

"Yes, may we see him?" asked Hank.

She hesitated. "Dr. Rogers wanted to speak with you first. If you'll come with me?"

They followed her down a long, sterile hallway, past dozens of glass-walled rooms. Unidentifiable patients, covered in bandages and life-saving equipment blended together, revealing neither their sex nor their age. Doris couldn't help but wonder if one of them might be Ben. Her son needed her. Couldn't Dr. Rogers wait?

The doctor greeted the couple as they entered a small office. "Please take a seat," he said.

Hank put a protective arm around Doris as a fresh set of tears flowed.

"We nearly lost the patient while you were in flight."

"By the patient, you mean Ben, our son?" asked Hank. It disturbed him that that doctor still didn't refer to Ben as a living, breathing person.

Dr. Rogers paused. "Yes, the patient suffered…"

"But Ben's all right now?" Doris interrupted.

"His condition is extremely serious," said Dr. Rogers. He switched on a light box and hung two images over it.

"These are the results from the patient's CT Scan. As you can easily see," he said, pointing to the irregular shape of the brain, "the patient has sustained a severe brain injury. But more importantly," he tapped several dark blotches, "he has several hematomas, or bleeding on his brain, which is causing it to swell. We need to get that swelling under control before it makes contact with his fixed skull. If that happens, there will be no chance of survival."

"What can we do?" asked Hank.

"Under normal conditions, we would drill a small hole into the skull to alleviate the pressure. But in your son's case, the swelling is so great that his brain would literally overflow his skull like soda fizzing out of a can."

Hank bristled at the graphic description, his distaste for Dr. Rogers growing stronger by the minute.

"But you can still do something, can't you?" pleaded Doris.

"Are you religious?" asked the Doctor.

She nodded, "We're Jewish."

"Then I suggest you pray."

Doris' nails dug into Hank's hand, as her shoulders shook with silent sobs. She felt as if she might die at any moment herself. Hank gave her a stern look. He had the distinct feeling Dr. Rogers got some kind of twisted pleasure out of other people's pain.

Doris tried to pull herself together. This wasn't about her. It was about Ben. Everything she was doing was for her son and she had to stay strong.

"We've got the patient on an ice mattress to help lower his body's temperature in hopes of bringing the swelling on his brain down and he's on the maximum dosage of medicine we can offer. There's nothing else we can do. The rest is up to him. The next three days are the most critical. We'll just have to watch and wait."

"I understand the odds are against Ben," Hank said, emphasizing his son's name, "but what if he does come out of his coma? What then? What will his life be like?"

Dr. Rogers shook his head. "I wouldn't count on it. If he makes it, it will be a miracle."

"I know, but what if?"

"Of course there are no hard and fast answers, but typically if a person is in a coma for an hour or less, they have mild brain damage and a corresponding disability."

"What kind of disability?" pressed Hank.

Dr. Rogers shrugged. "It's difficult to say. It all depends on what part of the brain was injured. Sometimes it's a physical disability, other times it's a mental disability, or possibly a combination of both."

"But Ben's been in a coma for longer," breathed Doris, dabbing her eyes.

"Yes, he has," agreed Dr. Rogers. "Patients in comas for one to twenty-four hours are considered to have moderate brain damage and disabilities."

"And after that?" asked Hank.

"Twenty-four hours or more and the damage will be severe. For each twenty-four-hour period after that, the damage and disabilities increase proportionately."

"Will he…will he be a vegetable?" whispered Doris.

Dr. Rogers frowned. It was rare for patients like this one to come out of a coma, and yet their families always played, "What if." It was a cruel game. It might be human nature to hold out hope, but it was always a slow and painful torture. Better to rip the Band-aid off quick, he always thought.

Aloud he said, "Don't get your hopes up. There is very little chance the patient will make it. Oftentimes in situations like these, even though the patient doesn't seem to respond to outside stimuli, they wait for their family members to arrive before they go."

"You didn't answer my wife's question."

Dr. Rogers studied Hank. He knew the man's bone structure intimately after hours of surgery on his son. He hoped Ben had the same steely resolve he now saw in his father's eyes. "To be honest, there's no way of knowing. All we can say is if he survives, brain damage is eminent."

The tears pooled in Doris' eyes. "He'll make it. Ben's a fighter," she nodded.

"All the same," cautioned Dr. Rogers, "you're asking for a miracle."

Hank nodded. "Then that's what we'll pray for."

Chapter Five

INTENSIVE CARE

A tangle of tubes, hoses, and wires encompassed Ben, as if a large robotic spider had woven a mechanical web around him. His left leg was ripped open in a four-inch-wide gash that ran from his knee to just below his ankle. His right leg also bore a large pear-shaped wound, so deep it exposed his fibula.

"This is a horrible nightmare," Doris said, burying her face in Hank's chest.

He hugged her tightly. As much as he wished she was right, there was no mistaking the young man in the bed. Had it only been three days since he'd waved good-bye to their son in the driveway?

"It is," he whispered.

Tears ran openly down her cheeks as she turned to look at her once strong child. His face was covered with so much dried blood that she might think he was dead if she hadn't been told otherwise.

Ben was still covered in dried blood from the accident. There was so much of it caked on his face, across his chest, and down his legs.

"Can't you clean him up?" Doris asked a nurse who'd come to check on Ben.

The pretty young woman nodded. "It was more important to stabilize his immediate injuries. We'll be cleaning him up soon, but we thought you might want a few minutes with him first."

There were huge steel halos attached to both of Ben's legs. Hank gingerly touched the cold metal fused to his child.

"They're called Hoffman devices," offered the nurse.

Long pins ran from the halos into Ben's skin. They twisted through his flesh to hold his shattered bones in place.

"Over time the pins are adjusted to make sure his bones heal properly," she explained.

Unable to find his voice, Hank nodded. He'd been warned it would be bad, but he doubted anything could have prepared him. No one ever expects to see their child on his deathbed.

A brace wound around Ben's torso to stabilize his broken clavicle. His arms were tied down to keep him from involuntarily flailing and injuring himself or pulling out one of the numerous IVs that sprang from his body.

The beeps of the heart and pulse monitors, combined with the hiss of the respirator, grew until they roared in Hank's ears. It was almost more than he could bear, until he reminded himself that those noises meant Ben was still alive. As long as they still beeped and hissed, there was hope.

Dr. Rogers stepped in, his face grim. "These next 24 hours are going to be critical for the patient. As I previously explained, if his brain makes contact with his fixed skull, he will not survive."

Hank nodded. "May I have a word with you out in the hallway?"

"Certainly." Dr. Rogers followed him into the corridor.

"A little while ago you told me that patients often wait to die until their loved ones arrive. That must mean no matter how bad the situation, there's awareness at some level. Therefore, I believe that somewhere deep inside him, Ben can hear you."

"We have no evidence to support..."

"Dr. Rogers," Hank interrupted, "you may not have scientific proof, but you've said it yourself. You've seen the evidence or you wouldn't have told us."

The doctor looked at Hank for a long minute. "I suppose you're right."

Hank nodded. With his Ph.D in Psychology, and his being a licensed marriage and family therapist, he firmly believed in the power of the mind. A simple shift in perspective or thought was often the breeding ground for a miracle. He'd witnessed numerous reversals of fortune through the power of positive thought. He had whole lists of people he helped who'd repaired marriages, become productive members of society, and overcome paralyzing fears and sicknesses just through shifting the focus of their thoughts to more positive grounds.

"From now on, Doctor, please call Ben by his name and act as if Ben can hear you. If you want to talk about low survival rates or his chances of waking up, please step out into the hall," Hank said.

Dr. Rogers frowned. "Chances are, he doesn't hear us."

"I'll take my chances that he does. In fact, my family would like to make a recording for Ben that we can play for him several times a day."

"It's highly unconventional."

"Unconventional maybe, but can it hurt?"

Dr. Rogers paused. It wouldn't hurt the…Ben, but he hated to see this family building themselves up on false hope. He locked eyes with Hank, who was giving him that steely look of resolution again.

"No," Dr. Rogers admitted, "it won't hurt." He was beginning to sense there was something different about this family.

CHAPTER SIX

MONTVALE

Back at the family home in Montvale, New Jersey, it was as if Ben had already died. Aunt Helga and Uncle Eddie, cousins Judy and Yair, and Ben's girlfriend Cassandra, took up vigil in the living room. Other friends and family dropped by with casseroles and covered dishes, then stayed to talk in hushed voices. The dark, warm clothing of early spring combined with the puffy, red eyes of so many guests added to the surreal, funerary atmosphere.

Every time the phone rang, the house went quiet. Though no one dared say it, they held their collective breath wondering the same thing: would this be the call saying Ben was gone?

Debbie and Michelle sat on the couch next to each other, poised to grab the receiver. They tried not to meet each other's eyes, for fear it would trigger fresh tears.

The phone blasted through the house like gunfire. Debbie grabbed for it with a shaky hand.

"I'm grabbing the extension," said Bruce, jogging into the other room.

"Hello?" Debbie answered, water welling in her eyes. "Aha," she sniffled, as the tears flooded her cheeks.

Their dad's voice was trembling. They had never heard him speak that way. He was always positive.

"Oh my G-d," Michelle whispered, hugging her sister's arm.

Debbie covered her eyes as she listened to her father and tried to ignore Bruce's breathing in the background. Their dad had always been such a positive, reassuring man. She knew Ben was in serious condition, but somehow their dad had always been able to make everything better.

It was silly to think he could fix this and yet the little girl inside her had thought he could.

Her heart sunk lower and lower as she listened. She'd fully expected encouraging news. The fact that he wasn't giving any chilled her to the bone. It meant things were really bad.

"Yes, I love you too," she said before replacing the receiver in the handset.

When she looked up, every set of eyes in the house was watching her. She cleared her throat. "Dad says Ben has irreversible brain damage. His brain is…" her voice broke. "His brain is bleeding and rapidly swelling. They don't ah, they don't think he's going to make it."

Loud wails of mourning went up throughout the house. Debbie and Michelle clung to each other crying uncontrollably.

Bruce rushed in. "What is the matter with everyone?" he seethed. "Shame on you! Shame on all of you. You're mourning him and acting as if Ben is already gone," he shouted above the weeping. "Ben is still here! It's not a time for mourning; it's a time for action. He needs our love and support. Our positive thoughts and prayers! Hope only dies when you let it. We will have a lifetime to mourn this loss if we don't focus and help my brother now."

"What can we do?" asked his girlfriend.

Michelle's eyes lit up. "We're going to make a recording for Ben." She ran out of the room as the bewildered guests stared after her.

"Let's give him positive encouraging messages," explained Bruce, "let him know how much he has to look forward to, how much we care, how much we miss him."

One by one the guests nodded.

"I've got it," Michelle said reappearing with the device. She clicked it on, then stopped, tears filling her eyes. "I um…I…" she looked weakly around the room, as everyone watched expectantly.

Debbie gently took the recorder and spoke into it. "We love you Ben."

Michelle wiped her eyes, then added, "You have to get better so that you can flirt with all those pretty nurses."

"You can't get lazy now," smiled Bruce taking the recorder from his sisters. "You have to fight. I promise you that before you know it, you and I will race and you will kick my ass and then joke with me that I was right when I made that recording for you. You have to fight, fight, fight."

* * *

Less than a hundred miles away, students and faculty at Trenton State College were also getting the news of Ben's accident...or at least Jack was trying to let them know.

"Come on, Anne, pick up," he whispered into the pay phone receiver.

This is Anne McGillis, director of student housing. If this is an emergency please hang up and dial campus police...

Jack impatiently waited for the rest of the recorded message to play through. He knew she lived somewhere on campus, but had no idea how to get a hold of her.

When the beep finally sounded, he could barely control his voice. "Anne, it's Jack." He swallowed. "Something has happened. Something really bad. Ben won't be..." his voice cracked as the reality that he would not be driving back to campus with his best friend sunk in. He cleared his throat. "Ben won't be coming back early to open up the dorm. You've got my number. Please give me a call as soon as you can."

He leaned his head back against the hospital wall and rubbed his eyes. He hadn't slept in more than 24 hours, but he didn't care. An image of Ben in his campus apartment filled Jack's head. His "big brother" was the youngest residence hall director in the history of Trenton State. The position as head of a dorm, overseeing several R.A.s, was usually reserved for graduate students, but Ben was such an outstanding R.A. that they'd made an exception when he was only a junior.

Ben and Jack had had more than a few laughs about how Ben often had to go break up older students' parties. But the coolest thing about Ben's director job was that he got his own apartment, complete with a kitchen and living room. They'd had several parties of their own there.

Anne, Ben's boss, had always been cool about it, as long as they kept a low profile. Jack really wished she would call. Anne and Ben were close friends. He didn't want her to hear about it from just anyone.

"Jack, where's Ben?"

Jack blinked. "Ralph, Ted, what are you doing here?"

27

Two of Ben's R.A.s were standing in the hospital hall with messy hair and exhausted looks on their faces. With their rumpled clothes and unshaven faces, they hadn't slept in quite a while either.

"We just had to come see Ben. Is he all right?"

"He's still in a coma. You must have driven all night. Who'd you get to watch the dorm on such short notice?"

The R.A.s looked at each other.

Jack shook his head. Because of their important duties, R.A.s weren't supposed to leave campus without permission from their director...in this case Ben. "You know you're going to be fired."

"I don't care," said Ralph. "It's worth it just to be able to see our good friend Ben."

Ted nodded. "Some things are more important than jobs."

"Still, you shouldn't have risked your job for Ben. He wouldn't have wanted you to do it," said Jack.

Ralph shrugged, "I'm not doing it for Ben, I'm doing it for me."

"All right then, I'll show you where he is. Just be prepared. He's in pretty bad shape."

Chapter Seven

THE WAIT

Doris and Hank first prayed that Ben would come out of the coma within 24 hours, but the window of opportunity quickly closed. Bruce arrived and played the recordings from home, but there was still no change. Another 24 hours passed, and then another, with similar results.

Doris sat in the room quietly watching Ben for the most microscopic of movements. She watched him so closely her eyes burned, yet she continued to stare, afraid she might miss the sign she'd been praying for.

Hank pulled a camera from his pocket. His voice sounded unusually loud in the glass-enclosed room.

"Do you think they'll let us?"

"Why not? He's our son." Hank said snapping a shot of Ben. "Besides, we might not have another chance and we need to document this." He snapped a second and third shot.

"He'll be fine. He'd want people to know. He probably will want to see them himself," he said with a catch in his voice. He hoped Ben would be able to see them one day.

Doris opened her purse and took out a notebook and pen.

"What are you doing?" asked Hank.

She looked at him with tear-filled eyes. "Writing."

"Did you forget something?"

"No. I may not be taking pictures like you do, but I can keep a diary. Ben will want to know what happened and I know I'll forget if I don't write it all down."

"I think he'll like that."

Doris wiped her eyes with the back of her hand, and continued to scribble. "I think we need to do something else too."

"What's that?"

"We need pictures of Ben, lots of pictures in here. I want these walls covered with his family and shots of him doing the things he loved best. That doctor might treat him like a nameless faceless number, but I want everyone who takes care of him, nurses, aides, technicians, to know him as a person. They need to know he's somebody special. Somebody who could be their son, brother, or best friend."

"I think that's a wonderful idea," said Hank hugging her. "I'll tell the kids to start going through photos when I call."

As the days ticked by, there was no change in Ben's condition. Bruce left his new job and flew down to help care for his brother.

"Are you sure you should be taking time off so soon?" asked Doris.

"It's okay Mom, there are thousands of jobs out there; I only have one brother," Bruce said, hugging her.

She furrowed her brow, torn between two sons. "You don't have to do this."

"It's all right," he smiled, "I want to."

She patted his cheek. "You're such a good brother."

"Look who raised me," he teased. "Now where do I put my bags?"

"Pastor Rehnquist has arranged a room for us in the hospital."

"A pastor? Does he know we're Jewish?"

Doris shook her head. "It's a service they offer to family members of severe trauma patients. Apparently they have a lot due to the Daytona 500 track and all the NASCAR and bike races."

Bruce picked up his bags and followed her down the hall. "Where's Dad?"

"He's making arrangements to go home."

"Home?" Bruce looked alarmed. "Has something happened?"

"No, but we don't know if…" she cleared her throat, "we don't know when Ben will wake up, and your dad has a practice to run." She pushed the door open to a room similar to those the patients used. Despite its sterile green walls and crisp white sheets on industrial metal bed frames, the place felt dirty to her. She'd already scrubbed it from floor to ceiling once. Hank thought her assessment of the accommodations was linked more to what was going on in their lives than the actual room. She supposed that was true, but cleaning it had also occupied her mind and made her feel useful.

Bruce set down his bags and hugged her. "It's going to be all right. We'll get through this together."

She nodded and whispered. "I think we're in for the long haul."

"There you are," said Hank coming down the hall. "My flight's all booked. I leave in five hours. Anyone care to join me in the cafeteria?"

Doris shook her head. "You two go. I'm going back down to Ben."

Hank cleared his throat. "Remember what I told you about keeping your strength up?"

She nodded. "Make sure to take some time for myself." She knew he was right, but she just couldn't bring herself to stay away from Ben for more than 15 minutes. It might not be logical, but she didn't think he would die while she was there. It would disappoint her too much and he was too loving to do that to her.

"I'll see you later," she said, checking her watch. It had been too long already.

Bruce followed Hank toward the elevator, but when they got around the corner his father stopped.

"What's wrong Dad?"

"Come with me, I need to tell you something."

They walked into an unoccupied, sunny waiting room.

"I didn't want to say anything in front of your mother, but I needed to tell someone."

"Dad, you're scaring me."

Hank nodded. "I know and I'm not trying to, but there's a strong possibility, your brother may not make it."

"No, no, he's Ben, he'll…"

"Let me finish," said Hank putting a hand on Bruce's shoulder. "Years ago, when your grandparents died, I purchased two graves for your mother and me."

Tears filled Bruce's eyes, "No, Dad."

Hank's voice caught, as he watched Bruce. "I hate like hell that I might have to use one for my own child, but if Ben…doesn't survive, some arrangements are already in place." He nodded more to himself, "I've already taken care of that."

"You won't have to use it, Dad," said Bruce hugging his father. "I'm going to take good care of Ben and Mom too. We'll all be waiting for you right here next weekend."

* * *

Doris taped the last of several dozen pictures to the wall. "There. What do you think?" she asked Bruce.

"Looks great, Mom."

She had created a collage of memories throughout Ben's room. The photos ranged from pictures of Ben as a baby, to shots of him riding his first bike, playing baseball, and blowing out candles on his birthday cake. There were others of him as a young adult: diving off a high dive, with his arms around his girlfriend Cassandra who he'd been dating for four years, others of him surrounded by plenty of friends and family.

"Wow, what are all these?" asked the nurse with the dark tan and blond streaked hair that had met them on the first day. Since then, Doris had learned that her name was Fiona and she was engaged to a firefighter. Doris felt that if she wanted everyone to get to know Ben, it was important she get to know the staff as well. So she'd made it a point to never call anyone "nurse" or "miss," but by their names.

"I thought you might like to see what kind of a person you're caring for," said Doris proudly as she watched Fiona move from shot to shot.

"He looks like quite the athlete," smiled Fiona.

Tears welled in Doris' eyes. "It's hard to keep Ben still. He's the type of guy who always has to be doing something."

Fiona smiled at the shots of Ben. "He looks like quite a character."

"He was very easy to raise, not moody like some babies. He's a very good person, very playful, with a goofy sense of humor, a little too vain, and quite the kibitzer."

"What's this?" asked Fiona peering at a shot of Ben obviously standing on his tiptoes next to a pretty girl with dark hair.

"That's one of my favorites," said Doris, wiping the corner of her eyes. "Ben's younger sister Michelle is taller than him, poor guy, so when he poses next to her, he fools around trying to appear taller than she is."

Fiona smiled. "It looks like you have a very charming son. I can't wait to meet him."

"I'm sure he'll like you too," said Doris. "Have you had breakfast yet?" she asked, offering Fiona a donut.

"Doris, you shouldn't have. I swear I gain 3 pounds every time I come by this room!"

"It's all right; you could use a little extra weight. All you Florida girls are too skinny."

Doris made a regular habit of bringing the nurses and other hospital workers donuts, candy, and flowers. She wasn't above bribing them to make sure Ben got the best care possible. If that meant showing a little extra gratitude so they enjoyed stopping by his room or came by more often, so be it.

Though there was little change in Ben's condition, Bruce and Doris spent the days in his room, just in case. They held his hand, played the recording from home, and talked to him.

"Remember how you begged Mom and Dad to let you play football freshman year?" Bruce asked Ben. "You wanted to be just like me, but you were always so much smaller."

Doris laughed.

"And then the first play of your first scrimmage, you broke your wrist! Guess you got that one beat now, huh?" He watched Ben's face, hoping for a slight reaction, but nothing happened.

"But you were determined to get back on the team. Man, you were like a dog with a bone. You wouldn't stop lobbying Mom and Dad until they gave you another shot the next year. You were a fighter then, and you're a fighter now," he gently squeezed Ben's hand. "I know you will pull through this."

Doris quietly got up and left the room. She wanted so badly to believe that Ben would wake up, but it had been eight days and she couldn't get Dr. Rogers' words out of her head. "Your son will most likely never regain consciousness. In most cases, their bodies just can't take the stress anymore and they eventually slip away."

Her definition of family had always been six. She had the perfect family, two sons, two daughters, and a husband. Five would never do. Tears filled her eyes. One of her kids predeceasing her was unthinkable, unacceptable!

She had worked her whole life to raise her children right. She'd fed them properly, kept them warm and healthy, taught them their ABCs, to avoid strangers and other dangers and in the blink of an eye, a thoughtless, stupid human being had undone all her hard work. How could the inconsiderate bastard have done this to her family? How could anyone with half a brain in their head let someone like that walk out of their bar, let alone get behind the wheel of his car? How could someone have done so much and walked away without even a scratch? Was he even aware of what he'd done? Did he even feel a shred of remorse? She'd asked Hank when she's talked with him the night before.

"We should make him come look at Ben, see his destruction first hand," she'd fumed.

"He doesn't deserve a minute of our attention," Hank reminded her. "We have to be prepared for what Ben will be like if he does wake up from this coma," he confided. "What if he has to spend the rest of his life in a nursing home? What if he comes home and needs around-the-clock care? How are we going to afford the astronomical medical bills? We might have to sell our house."

"Oh Hank, how can you even think about money at a time like this?" asked Doris.

"I'm sorry, but I can't help thinking what life might be like."

She knew Hank was wondering if he'd seen Ben alive for the last time. It killed him to go back to work, but he would do what he had to, to provide for his family. Right now this was how he could help Ben most.

Doris bit her lip. Hank had always been her rock. She wanted to lift his spirits and tried to think of something encouraging. The best she could come up with was, "We'll just have to cross that bridge when we come to it."

Chapter Eight

BLESSINGS

Doris sat in the special waiting room set aside for the families of severe trauma patients and wrote in her diary. Eight people used the quiet room, bound together by tragedy. She was glad to be away from the general waiting area where visitors talked in loud voices, babies cried, and various business personnel greeted each other in cheery voices. But she didn't relish being there either. She tried to avoid the room whenever possible, but sometimes circumstances necessitated she wait there. It was difficult enough to deal with her own heartbreak, let alone that of others.

Maybe it was denial, but she didn't see herself like those other people. Her son hadn't done anything wrong. He wasn't engaged in risky behavior or crazy stunts; he'd just been crossing the street.

Doris tried to reassure herself that it wouldn't be long before Eve came to get her to let her know they were through with Ben's latest round of tests.

A woman about Doris' age came into the room with tears streaming down her face.

"Mary?" Doris asked rushing to the mother of a young man who'd been in a motorcycle accident.

"He's gone," sobbed Mary.

Doris hugged her and began to cry with her. "It's all right," she said rocking her. "We'll get through this." Her heart felt as if it were about to explode in her chest. How could such a bright, healthy young man be there laughing and so full of life one minute and gone the next? She'd never understand how such terrible things could happen. It was a living nightmare and if it could happen to Mary and her son, it could happen to Ben. The thought sent a chill up Doris' spine as she continued to cry and rock Mary.

"Is there anyone I can call for you?" she asked quietly.

The woman handed her a slip of paper with several names.

"Don't worry about a thing," said Doris helping her new friend to a chair. "Sit here as long as you need to and I'll take care of everything."

Doris took a deep breath and walked out into the hall. After today she vowed never to use the waiting room again. Her heart couldn't take it anymore.

"Doris, what's wrong?" asked a familiar voice behind her.

"Hank!" She said flying into his arms, "I didn't think you'd be here until later."

"I got an earlier flight. Is everything ok?"

"Ben's fine, but Mary's son didn't make it,"

Hank's eyes softened. "Oh, I'm sorry. Things looked so promising for them."

Doris' eyes began to cloud again. "It's a living nightmare. If he couldn't make it, what about Ben?"

Hank wiped her cheeks. "You mustn't think that way. The two things are completely unrelated."

"I know, I know, but I can't help it. Every time I think about that, that senseless, stupid man who hurt our son, I want to kill him!" Her eyes were blazing. "I know it's wrong, but I wish he were dead. If he were right here, I'd kill him myself. And Hank, you know I'm not the violent type, but I swear if I ever got ahold of him," she hit her fist in her palm. "I don't think there's a court in the country that would convict me."

Hank nodded. "I know what you mean. I've told a few of my patients about the accident. One of them did a little checking on the driver. Turns out this isn't the first time he's done something like this. He spent a few years in the pen for killing two women and severely injuring another passenger."

Doris inhaled sharply. "You mean he killed others and they still let him out of prison?"

"Apparently drunk driving doesn't carry a very stiff sentence in Florida."

"Death's too good for him," said Doris between gritted teeth.

* * *

"I wanted to introduce myself to you," smiled a middle-aged, balding doctor. "I'm Sol Levinson, the neurosurgeon that will be working with Ben."

Doris smiled. She liked this man much better than Dr. Rogers already. "Has there been a change in Ben's condition?"

"Not yet, but I always tell my patients and their families not to give up hope."

"Then why are you working with Ben?"

"Dr. Rogers is our trauma surgeon. He works with emergency causes. Because Ben has been here for several days now, he's been transferred to my care."

Tears of relief welled in Doris' eyes. Finally someone was going to be taking care of her son, the way she wanted. "Would you like some candy?" she said, offering him the new box of chocolates she'd just bought in the gift shop.

"Caramel squares, my favorite," he said, taking one. "Tell me about Ben. I understand you've made a special audiotape for him. Does he seem to respond to it?"

"We hold his hand all the time. When it's on I could swear it feels like he's squeezing me back."

Dr. Levinson made a few notes on Ben's chart. "Well he certainly looks healthy considering all he's been through."

"So you think he'll wake up?"

Dr. Levinson shrugged. "The human body is a remarkable thing. I have patients with impossible odds against them that surprise me every day. There's no reason Ben shouldn't be one of them."

Doris liked that prediction. She couldn't wait until Hank got back to tell him about their new and improved doctor!

CHAPTER NINE

DAY TEN

Far-off beeps and a growing hissing sound drifted into Ben's awareness. The heavy weight of deep sleep loosened its grip on him, sending him floating into a lighter place. He could see the brightness through the reds of his eyelids. He wanted to open them, but it was nearly impossible. The fleeting thought that someone had super-glued them shut crossed his mind. He tried again, and they opened a fraction.

The room was blurry. Someone nearby said something to him, but it sounded like they were underwater.

Slowly a young man and older woman came into focus; their smiling faces inches from his. He tried to back away, but couldn't move.

"Relax. It's going to be ok. Just stay calm," said the excited man.

Tears streamed down the woman's face as she hugged Ben. "Everything's going to be alright now. I love you so much."

The young man and older woman disappeared and were replaced by an older man. He took out a flashlight and shined it in Ben's eyes. "Can you hear me? Do you know what your name is? Do you know the year? Who is president? Can you feel this? What about this?"

Ben tried to answer the questions, but his throat was dry and parched. It was difficult to say anything. He tried to lift his arms, to move the man back, but realized they were tied down. Who would tie down his arms? Why was everything so difficult?

Loud noises went off as people rushed in and out of the room. A burning, crushing pain crept up his legs. The room began to spin. Ben briefly closed his eyes to get his bearings.

What was going on? Why was everyone acting so strange?

"It's a miracle," said the young man coming back into Ben's line of sight. Tears glistened in his eyes. He squeezed Ben's hand. "You were in a very bad car accident. We nearly lost you."

Ben closed his eyes again. If he was in a car accident he must have been driving. He always preferred to drive. His eyes flashed open in alarm. Who else had been hurt? Had he killed someone? Someone in his family? A friend? A kid on the street? He struggled to get someone's attention but the older man with the light was clearing the others out.

"Relax and get some rest," said the man patting his arm. "You've had quite a rough 10 days."

"Ten days! " Where was he? Ben struggled to remember how he got there, but it was all a big blank. The last thing he recalled was leaving for spring break. Someone had come with him. Who was it?

His heart pounded in his chest. Jack! Jack must have been with him. Had he killed his best friend? Where was he? He had to get answers, but everyone had left his room.

Why hadn't they told him what had happened? Were they trying to spare him the pain? What didn't they want him to know?

Panic rose in the pit of his stomach, worse than the pain that burned in his legs. How could he live with himself? They should have left him on the roadside. He didn't think he could go on. He didn't deserve to go on.

A single tear fell as he closed his eyes. He was so ashamed of himself. How could he have been so reckless? He hated himself for causing such pain. He doubted he could ever face his fraternity brothers again.

Chapter Ten

THE LONG ROAD

"I need you to take a deep breath and blow," Fiona instructed Ben. He did as he was told so that she could pull his respirator out. He coughed and gagged, taking in huge gulps of air on his own for the first time in nearly two weeks.

Hank and Debbie had flown down for the big event. Ben hadn't been able to talk with the tube down his throat so he'd mostly nodded or shook his head, even when he wasn't sure what they were saying. His responses made them so happy; he didn't have the heart to let them down.

His brain felt like scrambled eggs. To be honest, he didn't recognize the people who visited him. He'd been told they were his family. They seemed nice enough and genuinely concerned, so he continued to see them.

"What's your name?" asked Dr. Levinson, once the tube had been removed.

Ben's throat felt like sandpaper. He let out a whistling sound and coughed.

The nurse held a cup of water to his lips and he sipped.

"Just relax and tell us your name," coached the Doctor.

"Hershel Walker," croaked Ben.

Hank and Doris exchanged looks. He was their son's favorite football player. Maybe he'd misunderstood the question. Doris made a note in her diary.

"Can you repeat your name again?" Hank asked.

"Hershel Walker, the ideal American," rasped Ben.

"Can you tell us how old you are?" asked the physician.

Ben blinked, why were they asking such ridiculous questions? "180."

"How much do you weigh?" questioned Dr. Levinson.

"About a thousand pounds."

"Do you know who I am?" Debbie asked, stepping up to the bed.

She looked familiar, but he couldn't quite place her. "My girlfriend?"

"Ben," Hank leaned into his son's line of sight, "can you tell me what fraternity you belong to?"

"Theta Chi."

"Where did you go to high school?"

"Pascack Hills."

"Thank you," encouraged the doctor. "Go ahead and rest, I'm going to speak with your family."

Ben lay back on his pillow. He wondered if he would be allowed to eat now that the respirator was out. He couldn't remember when the last time he'd had food was.

Dr. Levinson closed the door to Ben's room. "Your son is exhibiting all the signs of severe brain damage. He doesn't know his own name, recognize his family, or have any concept of measurements."

"How can you say that?" asked Hank. "He responds to his name and he seems to have retained some long-term memory."

"He's quite fortunate to have any memory at all, or speech for that matter," nodded Dr. Levinson.

"How long will it take him to get his memory back?" asked Doris.

The doctor shook his head. "Severe brain damage is irreversible. He might make some improvements, but the physical damage to his brain will never get better. One of my favorite quotes is 'touch the brain, never the same'"

"But Dr. Rogers said he wouldn't wake up either," she pointed out.

"He did beat the odds."

"So there's a chance he'll get better also," she continued.

"No, the brain doesn't work that way. It doesn't regenerate."

"Well then, Ben will just learn to use different parts of his brain," Hank said with confidence.

"That would be very unusual," said Dr. Levinson. "The best thing you can do for your son is to be realistic. Accept his condition and start planning for it. He's going to need a great deal of help without his short-term memory. And remember, we don't know the full extent of his injuries yet."

"What do you mean?" swallowed Doris as the familiar heat of tears gathered behind her eyes. "I thought Ben was getting better."

"In some ways, yes. But with the damage to his brain stem, he may never be, never regain balance, coordination, or the ability to walk again."

"Then I guess we better pray for a few more miracles," choked Doris.

Dr. Levinson nodded. Ben and his family would need more than a few miracles; they'd need an entire truckload. But if anyone could accomplish it, it was Ben. Even Dr. Levinson didn't believe Ben would survive the injuries from the accident and wake up out of the coma. The human body never ceased to amaze him.

Chapter Eleven

CONVERSATIONS

It had been two days since the respirator had come out and Ben was restless. He'd never been the type to lie on his back and watch the world pass him by. Or was he? He couldn't remember.

There was a button to adjust the bed, but it really didn't matter. The scenery was much the same in one position as the other. He needed something to distract him from the aching pain in his legs. It felt as if someone had taken a sledge hammer to them.

Though he couldn't remember much, his tortured legs wouldn't let him forget he had Compartment Syndrome. His unbelievable agony was a side effect of the serious disorder, which caused disproportionate pain that couldn't be controlled with even the strongest painkillers.

The pain was so excruciating that he couldn't help screaming as wave upon wave of pain washed over him. He knew he must sound like a whining baby, but he couldn't help himself. It was like a constant branding iron searing into his flesh while simultaneously twisting deeper. He'd often wake himself up in the night with his own screams.

"I brought you something," smiled a familiar, tall girl, after a particularly painful and restless night.

Ben smiled back. "I know I should know you," he said slowly.

"That's all right. I'm your sister, Michelle."

"Michelle," he said trying to force his brain to remember her the next time.

She held up a fuzzy, yellow, moon with a smiley face on it.

"You brought me a stuffed animal?"

"Not just any stuffed animal. This one will help you with your pain," she said putting it into his hand. "Any time you feel pain coming, give this guy a squeeze and it will help keep the worst of it under control."

As if mentioning pain awakened Ben's Compartment Syndrome, he was hit with another sharp spasm. "Ohhhh" he moaned.

"Squeeze," Michelle encouraged him.

He grasped the moon with all his strength and squeezed and squeezed until all he could feel was the squeeze. When he finally stopped the pain was gone.

"That's great," he panted, out of breath. "What made you think of this?"

Michelle laughed. "I don't know if I should tell you this."

"What's that?"

"It's one of the things they teach women to do in birthing classes to help control their contractions."

Ben let out a robotic sounding laugh. "Well, it works."

He kept the stuffed moon under his blankets, close enough so that he could reach it at all times but far enough out of sight to keep people from thinking he needed a "security blanket."

Though he hoped he would need it less over time, the pain in his legs continued to increase. Within days, his left leg developed Methicillin Resistant Staph, or M.R.S.A, a serious hospital-borne infection. It was easy to contract, difficult to treat, and nearly impossible to get rid of. Worst of all, if it wasn't kept under control, he could lose his leg.

Ben had already had multiple reconstructive surgeries and skin grafts to cover the open wounds on his legs. Yet the grafts hadn't taken, which left the deep gashes in his legs painfully exposed—increasing the opportunity for the M.R.S.A. to spread. It also meant he had to have more, increasingly painful surgeries.

But his problems didn't end there. He tried to watch TV to provide a needed distraction from his ongoing pain. The problem was that Ben couldn't follow an entire TV show without forgetting what it was about. When he picked up a magazine to read, he was reminded that his reading comprehension was completely shot. He recognized letters and words and could even read them aloud in whole sentences and paragraphs, but by the time he finished reading, he had no idea what he just read. Even when he tried to carry on a conversation, he couldn't remember and use common words that he knew were somewhere in his vocabulary. Other times he would try to have a conversation, but would keep forgetting what it was about when it was his turn to respond.

"Is it almost time for lunch?" he asked when Doris walked in with a fresh box of donuts for the nurses.

"You just ate fifteen minutes ago, remember?"

He looked at her. "I did?"

His words were monotone, though she knew he meant it as a question. Ben had always been so animated. It was difficult to hear him speak without energy or emotion. She wondered if the part of his brain that controlled inflection had been damaged. Was that why he spoke without any affect or personality?

She tried not to show her concern as she smiled and fluffed his pillows. "Bruce gave you chocolate ice cream. You fussed because you said he shouldn't have to waste his time feeding you."

Ben looked down, noticing the clavicle brace, which made it difficult to move as well as the IVs and equipment running in and out of his arms. "He shouldn't have to. No one should have to feed me," he said in a robotic voice.

"Nonsense, there's no reason to have a staff member do it when you've got your family right here."

Ben shifted slightly. The pain was getting to him again. He couldn't bear to look at his mangled legs. It shocked him every time he saw them. It also made him think of what he must have done. Who had he killed? His stomach churned until he thought he might puke.

Doris fanned him with an envelope she'd been carrying. "Relax, relax, you're okay. Everything's going to be just fine."

Ben took a few deep breaths forcing back bile. How could she be so nice to him after what he'd done?

"Look, something came from home for you," she said holding the envelope still in front of him.

He stared at the neat black type. "University of Bridgeport School of Law," he said without emotion.

Doris opened it and held it out to him. "It's an acceptance letter. You got into law school!"

Ben gave her a sad smile. With his lack of reading comprehension, there was no way he could even finish the last six weeks of college, let alone attend law school. He yawned as his Swiss cheese mind began to drift.

"Is it time for lunch yet?"

* * *

"Mom" Michelle knocked on Doris' door. "May I come in?"

Doris was sitting by the window in her hospital room writing in the diary, which had become her constant companion.

"Yes, sweetheart, what do you need?"

Michelle sat on the edge of the bed. "He's not the same, is he?"

"No, but his recovery's just started."

Michelle's eyes watered. "He didn't even know who I was."

Doris slid over to her daughter and put an arm around her. "He will, he will. Just give him some time."

"Oh Mom, what am I going to do?" cried Michelle. "I've always looked up to him and now he's gone."

Doris wiped the tears from under Michelle's eyes with her thumbs. "You still have him as your brother."

Michelle sniffed. "But it's not the same. I don't know what to do without him."

"What do you mean? Of course you do, you're a strong, independent, young woman."

"I know I am, but I've spent my whole life following Ben. When he had a paper route, I then had a paper route. When he took karate, I took karate. When he became a lifeguard, so did I. The list goes on!"

"I thought you did those things because you wanted to."

"Yes, of course I did, but I didn't know I wanted to do many of those things until Ben did it first and set an example. Now I've lost him as my older brother role model."

Doris patted her hand. "Then you need to look at Ben's accident as a gift."

Michelle's eyes widened. "I can't do that."

"He would never wish what happened to him on anybody, but I know that he would want some good to come out of it. And I know that he would tell you the same thing I'm going to tell you."

Michelle wiped a stray tear. "What's that?"

"That he has always been so proud of your many accomplishments and that you shouldn't let the sadness of his tragedy slow you down one bit. Ben has always been a fighter and he would want you to continue to be the exact same way."

Chapter Twelve

RELIEF

It had been nearly 10 days since Ben woke from his coma. He'd been transferred from the ICU to a regular hospital room. Though it meant his condition was improving and he was no longer in danger, he couldn't have felt worse. Guilt was nearly consuming him.

"Check out the new pad," joked Bruce when he came to check on Ben shortly after the room change.

Ben turned his head on his pillow, looking pale and miserable.

"Hey buddy, what's going on?" Bruce asked pulling up a chair to the bedside.

"What am I going to do?" Ben whispered.

His brother quirked a brow. "Do? About what?"

Ben shook his head. He couldn't bring himself to look at Bruce. His brother had left a very lucrative first job out of college to be with him. How could he be so kind? How could everyone be so kind to him when he was a killer?

"Do about what?" Bruce asked again.

Ben gulped. "I just don't know how I will ever face Jack's parents."

Bruce frowned. It was so hard to tell what was going on in his brother's scrambled egg brain. Sometimes he was perfectly rational and at others he sounded like a senile old man. "Why would you need to face Jack's parents?"

Tears began to run down Ben's face. "Because I killed him."

"Ben, you didn't kill anyone. Why would you even think that?"

"But the car accident, wasn't I driving?"

"You don't remember what happened?"

Ben shook his head.

"Geeze," Bruce paced. "And all this time no one told you?"

"I thought no one wanted to give me more bad news."

"Well I've got news for you. A drunk driver hit you while you were crossing the street. That's as bad as it gets."

"And Jack?"

"Is just fine. And so are the rest of your fraternity brothers."

A smile washed over Ben's face; the first genuine smile he had since waking. The weight that crushed his chest instantly disappeared. He hadn't killed anyone. He wasn't a murderer!

"What about the driver? What happened to him?" Ben asked.

"Walked away without a scratch. The police took him to jail."

"What's going to happen to him?"

"I don't know. Dad says what's important is you. We can deal with him later."

Ben closed his eyes and seemed to drift off to sleep. Bruce shook his head as he sat down. He couldn't believe no one had bothered to tell Ben what had happened. They might have been the ones with brain damage instead of the other way around. A lot of accident victims didn't remember what happened to them. With everything that had happened to Ben and all the things he was having trouble with now, it made sense that he had no memory of the accident.

"What about Jack?" Ben suddenly asked.

"What about him?"

"If he's fine, why hasn't he come to see me?"

"He's back at school in New Jersey. We're still in Florida, remember?"

There was a long silence as Ben tried to straighten his jumbled mind. "And my car is fine?"

"Your Trans Am's just fine. I'll take good care of it for you."

"Good," said Ben closing his eyes again. "I'm going to need to take it out next week."

Bruce couldn't tell if Ben was joking or just talking crazy again. Ben made a snoring sound and Bruce thought he might be down for the count when he opened his eyes again.

"Tell me about myself. What was I like? I don't remember much."

Bruce hesitated. He wasn't sure if he should. He'd seen plenty of shows in which doctors advised against people telling amnesia patients about past events, in favor of them remembering on their own. But no one had said anything about amnesia with Ben. His brother had brain damage.

He supposed it would be all right to share just a little of Ben's past life. For all either of them knew, Ben might forget it all in five minutes.

"You loved to run. Do you remember that?"

Ben shook his head.

Bruce smiled. "Well you did. In fact it was a dream of yours to run the mile in under six minutes. You used to train for hours, before and after school. Then just a few weeks ago you did it."

"I did?"

"Yes. You took part in the American Cancer Society Race back home."

"And I ran in under six minutes?" Ben asked in a monotone voice.

"You did it in five minutes and fifty seconds. You not only surpassed your goal, you won the race!"

Ben made a robotic sound that Bruce guessed was a chuckle.

"What do you know? I'm fast."

"The fastest," laughed Bruce. "You know what I think?"

Ben shook his head.

Tears glistened in Bruce's eyes. "I think that same determination you showed in mastering the mile in under six minutes is going to help you get through this too."

CHAPTER THIRTEEN

MIND MELDING

With Ben out of the I.C.U., Bruce decided to take a needed drive alongside the beach to clear his mind. It was dark and even though it was not raining, there was a lightning storm that night. Then Bruce suddenly started to get worried. He had this strong feeling that he needed to be back at the hospital immediately. A part of him felt that something was terribly wrong with Ben. He turned the car around and headed directly back to the hospital.

Bruce parked the car in the hospital lot. Before walking to the entrance, he briefly stopped and began to pray out loud during the simultaneous lightening storm overhead. "G-d, please strike me dead right now and in return just save my brother!"

Bruce then rushed through the hospital lobby directly to the elevator up to Ben's floor.

When he walked into Ben's room, he was initially relieved when he saw his brother. He carefully watched Ben to reassure himself that he was still breathing.

"Hey bro, it's time to wake up." Bruce said as he walked closer to Ben, who did not open his eyes. Bruce decided to gently nudge his shoulder. "C'mon big guy, it's time to wake up" he said, while gradually raising his voice.

But Ben didn't stir. Bruce became nervous and shook Ben a bit harder, "Time to get up, Ben. We have your favorite food."

Bruce then touched Ben's forehead. It was burning hot. "He's burning up! Call a doctor!" Bruce shouted to get the attention of the nurses in the hallway.

Ben remained silent and motionless. Within moments, several nurses were in the room working over him, taking his temperature, blood pressure, and performing other tests as they waited for a doctor.

"He won't wake up. He's running a high fever. It's up to 104.2 degrees. We've got to call the doctor STAT!" Bunny exclaimed over her shoulder as they continued to try to wake Ben.

Bruce walked up to the Ben's bed, unsure of what to do next, but sure that he could do something. "Come on Ben, time to get up. Stop messing with us and open those baby browns."

Bruce's mind was racing. He couldn't lose Ben now. Not after he'd come so far. There had to be something, some trigger that would get his brother to open his eyes and get better.

If only I could touch him and make him better, thought Bruce. A picture of Spock, from Star Trek, doing the Vulcan Mind Meld flicked through his head. Spock would simply place his hands on the temples of his subject and through intense powers of suggestion deduct the information or behavior he needed from them.

Why not? Thought Bruce. Nothing else was working. It might even make Ben laugh, if he was listening at some level.

Bruce leaned over Ben and placed his hands on either side of Ben's head, which seemed to get hotter by the minute. He concentrated on seeing a picture of energy flowing out of his hands and into Ben. He then lowered his head even with his brother's.

"Ben, you need to hear me now," he said in a stern voice. "I'm doing the Vulcan Mind Meld on you. I am willing you to wake up. When I count to three you will be awake. One, two, three."

Ben groggily opened his eyes.

"It worked!" gasped Bunny. "But how?"

"Does it matter?" asked Grace, checking Ben's vital signs again.

"I'll take it from here," said the doctor.

Bunny popped a piece of candy in her mouth from the dish Doris always kept full and continued to watch Ben in wonder while the doctor checked his extremities for swelling, listened to Ben's heart and lungs, then shone a light into his eyes, all the while quizzing the nurses on the latest information about his patient.

Ben's forehead glistened with sweat and he moaned softly during the examination. He felt disoriented and dizzy as if he were drunk.

"Ok, let's schedule him for surgery immediately," ordered the doctor.

"What's going on with my body?" Ben asked as he was watching the commotion around him.

"It looks like you have some blood clots in your legs and lungs, which is causing a pulmonary embolism. We need to operate as soon as possible to remove them or you could die," the doctor explained to Ben in a matter-of-fact way.

Ben's heart jumped into his throat. "Am I going to die?"

"Of all the questions to ask me," said the doctor with a half smile.

"Am I?" Ben asked again.

Dr. Levinson sobered. "You have a fifty-fifty chance. But Dr. Green is very good at what he does. So you are in excellent hands. After some initial tests, you will be his first surgery tomorrow morning."

Even though Ben was much closer to death in the early days following the accident, his being in a coma didn't allow him to consciously be aware of his condition. This was much scarier. His brain worked overtime trying to process the information that he just heard from the doctor.

Ben was relocated back to the I.C.U. He had forgotten how much busier the I.C.U. floor was as compared to the uneventful private room he had temporarily been in.

He wondered if these were his last few hours on earth? He didn't feel like he was dying, but the doctor said that his chances were "fifty-fifty." As he was lying in bed trying to fall asleep, he couldn't help wondering if he would wake up in the morning. Once they put him under anesthesia in the morning, would he ever wake up again? Ben barely slept that night.

"Wake up Ben, we need to run some tests before being brought to surgery," Ben heard as a nurse was waking him up the following morning. Doris was also in the room, and although she was trying to mask it from Ben, she looked very nervous.

"Don't worry Mom, I promise you that I won't die. I'm pretty confident that I'm going to make it."

"You better. In fact, if you promise to survive this ordeal, I'll even quit smoking," Doris said as she was holding Ben's hand. Ben was delighted to hear his mother make that promise. Throughout his entire life, he and his family tried everything to get Doris to stop smoking, but nothing ever worked.

"We've got a deal Mom," Ben replied as he was being wheeled away for tests and then to the operating room.

It felt like his heart would explode in his chest as the anesthesiologist lowered a mask over his nose and mouth.

"Just relax and count backwards with me," the man with kind blue eyes instructed.

But Ben fought it. He wanted to remain awake as long as he possibly could. These might be his final few glimpses of life. As much as he tried, he was out in a matter of seconds.

The surgery to remove the clot and implant the metal Greenfield Filter, a device that would prevent blood clots from entering the heart, took approximately four hours. Doctors first attempted to remove several clots manually. They cut an 18-inch incision in his lower left leg and flushed the area.

The surgeon then carefully made an incision into Ben's neck.

"I'm going to lead the filter through the jugular and place it near the heart," Dr. Green informed his assisting surgical intern. The student leaned in closer for a good look. But as the doctor started to thread the filter, Ben began to move his head.

"Hold him, hold him," ordered Dr. Green.

The anesthesiologist rechecked Ben's vitals, to make sure he was fully out. But the movements were involuntary. Ben continued to thrash, making it difficult and dangerous to continue the tedious procedure.

"New plan team," said Dr. Green closing the incision in Ben's neck. "Let's prep his groin. We're going in through the femoral artery."

Working like a well-oiled machine, the team made needed adjustments and maneuvered into their new positions in a matter of seconds. The rest of the surgery continued without incident.

In a matter of days, Ben was out of intensive care unit and back in a private room. Though he was physically getting better, depression began to set in. He began to think about all that he'd lost, and all he was missing out on. He worried about what he would do when he got out of the hospital. No one, not even his parents, knew the full extent of his brain damage. He couldn't hide some of his crazy responses, but they had no idea he couldn't comprehend the things they explained to him, what he read, or that his writing was like that of a first grader.

He hated the way his body looked. Once in peak physical condition and well muscled, he was wasting away. An ugly scar had formed over his left eye, which he thought made him look like a monster. He refused to look in a mirror anymore.

Most of all he hated his legs. They were grotesque. The grafts looked like the clear plastic wrap used to cover food, with the muscles and bones visible beneath the thin layer of skin.

But worst of all was the pain. As he continued to recover and become more lucid, he also gained more feeling in his limbs. Along with the feeling, came constant, excruciating discomfort. He could feel the metal bars from the Hoffman Devices, the twenty-pound halos on each leg, which were rammed through his legs. The pain started with a throbbing that grew until it wound its way up and around his legs, making them feel as if they were on fire. The torture ran together, blending in one all-consuming incubator of agony. It made communication nearly impossible, blindsiding his already impaired mind, so that he could barely concentrate.

The worst of the pain came three times a day, when his legs would be lifted so that the Hoffman Devices could be cleaned. To ward off further infection, the areas where the spoke-like nails connected with his skin were wiped down with rubbing alcohol. The lifting of his legs and the burning was excruciating beyond belief. He'd tried everything from begging to cut down on the number of cleanings to various distraction techniques, but relief evaded him. The cleanings always ended in screams of torment. When the seven-minute cleaning procedure was finished, he'd collapse, being physically and mentally exhausted.

Whenever Ben was asked how he was feeling, he'd have the same answer, "Not feeling pain is the exception." He wasn't trying to be coy or funny. It was the truth. Torturous pain gripped his every second of every minute, with limited moments of relief. The relief usually came after waking from surgery, savoring the lingering effects of anesthesia, or shortly after receiving pain medication.

It wasn't that the staff liked to see him in pain, but Ben was receiving the maximum dosages of painkillers allowed. Any more and he risked addiction.

He thought about his being so young and doubted an older person could have withstood the brutal, continuous pain that he endured. He seriously considered asking the doctors to simply amputate his left leg which was giving him the most pain, but he feared that he would realize soon after the surgery that the pain would still be there.

His uncle Eddie had lost his leg to cancer when he was in his twenties. Eddie had talked about phantom pains. At the time, Ben couldn't understand how you could feel something that was no longer there. Now he wondered if it was really his legs that gave him the pain or was his brain playing a similar trick on him, as Eddie experienced, making him feel pain that shouldn't exist.

The emotional burden of dealing with his mental and physical injuries became too much to bear. Ben spiraled further and further down into a deep hole of despair. He disassociated so much that when the doctors talked to him about his condition or upcoming surgeries, he'd stare at them blankly, without consideration for what they were really saying. It always sounded like they were talking about someone else. He couldn't fathom all the big words, let alone complicated procedures. At times, it almost sounded like they were building a cyborg. They couldn't possibly mean him. This was not his life.

Chapter Fourteen

THE PROMISE

Nearly five weeks had passed since Ben first came to Halifax Medical Center, but it felt more like five years to him. He thought it was a terrible mistake to put clocks in rooms with long-term patients like him. With little to do, he often found himself watching as the hands wound around the clock in a never-ending circle. Tick, tick, tick. Watching something like that only made the days go by even more slowly, especially given his continuous and horrendous pain.

Ben wished with all his heart that he could just get up and walk out of his room, that the nightmare would evaporate, and he could get on with his life. He'd been happy doing what he did before the accident, not like so many of his friends who couldn't wait to leave New Jersey or get out on their own with real jobs. He wondered if they realized how very lucky they were to have all that they did. He'd give anything to be able to have that life back again.

As he lay there thinking about all he'd lost and what he might never have again, he made a promise.

"Please G-d," he whispered into the quiet of his dark room. "I know I don't talk to you as much as I should, but I promise…no, I swear to you, that if you give me my life back…if I can be healthy and walk again, read right, talk, and finish school like I'm supposed to, I will do whatever I can to put an end to drunk driving. I still can't believe a drunk driver did all this to me. I will work for the rest of my life ending drinking and driving if I have to." He stopped to listen as the clock slowly ticked off the minutes. He wasn't sure what was supposed to happen, but it felt like something should.

"Do you hear me?" he called into the night. "I will work for the rest of my life to end drunk driving, if you would please give me my life back."

Nurse Grace poked her head in the door. "Were you calling me?"

Ben shook his head. "You must be hearing things."

She gave him a strange look and left.

"If we have a deal, send me a sign," said Ben into the sanctuary of his room.

"Isn't that what faith is all about?" asked Pastor Rehnquist coming into Ben's room.

Ben blushed. "I didn't think anyone could hear me."

"You didn't? Then why did you ask?"

Ben stared at the pastor for a moment. "Because I really want it."

"Then G-d will answer you."

"How do you know?"

"Because G-d always answers your prayers."

Ben frowned. He'd heard plenty of horror stories about other patients in the trauma unit. "Then why do people die? My mom's prayed with plenty of families who've come through here."

The pastor raised his brows. "G-d always answers prayers. We just don't always like his answers."

"Then what's the point?"

"The point is to do your part and have faith."

"And then what?"

"Know that G-d will give you exactly what you need to become the person you were meant to be."

Ben wasn't sure he had the kind of faith Pastor Rehnquist spoke of, but he never forgot the promise he made.

After a few weeks, Ben began to remember more and more leading up to the accident and often played the *what if* game. What if the guys in the bar had decided to fight him? Most likely his friends would have joined in and they would have torn the place up. It's possible he might have gotten a black eye or a bloody lip. They might even have been kicked out of the bar. Or he would have been arrested. But he was certain it would have delayed things long enough for the drunk driver to have zoomed down Ocean Avenue without either ever becoming aware of the other.

But then what if he hadn't hit Ben? What if he'd continued on down the street and hit a group of young women or a car with a family with kids? Would their smaller bodies have been able to withstand the impact? Did that car hitting him mean other people further on down the road spared death and were still alive?

And what if Ben had never gone on vacation to begin with? There was a point when he'd thought he'd outgrown the whole scene. He'd seriously thought about not going. Did his subconscious somehow know what was going to happen to him? Had it been trying to tell him something he was too busy to listen to?

Hank had walked in on him during one such game. "What are you thinking about?" he'd asked, pulling up a chair.

"Dad, do you ever wonder what would have happened if I hadn't come down here at all?"

"All the time. I often blame myself. You had reservations about going because you thought you outgrew the college spring break experience."

"You know you couldn't have stopped me."

"No, I couldn't have," Hank paused. "Do you remember that conversation about spring break before the accident?"

"I think so. You told me I should go. That it was important to have one last fling as a college student."

"I've often thought to myself, I shouldn't have encouraged you."

"Then why did you?"

"It's a rite of passage. You would have regretted not taking that opportunity. You probably would have spent the whole spring break, or possibly the years to come playing the very same *what if* game."

"I might have," agreed Ben. "But that's still much better than where I am now."

"Maybe, maybe not. There's no way of knowing. None of us have crystal balls. You could have spent another day on the beach and ended up drowning, or been killed in an accident on the way home. A second or two sooner and all three of you might have been hit and killed. Or maybe by this happening, and your mom and me coming down here, you've helped us avoid our own injury or accident. There's just no way to know what life will bring."

"So what can we do?"

"Do exactly what we did. Follow our hearts and do what is right for us now, so that we live with as few regrets as possible."

"And what if we still have regrets?"

"Then we learn from them."

"But I couldn't have helped what happened to me. There was no way of knowing that a drunk driver was coming down the street."

"No, there wasn't," Hank rubbed Ben's shoulder. "So why are you beating yourself up playing the *what if* game?"

"I…," Ben paused and looked at his father, "because I don't like where I am and I wish things were different."

Hank nodded. "So do I, but we can't fix that. All we can do is stay in the moment, learn from it, and respond as best we can. You don't see the things I do, because you're here every day, but each time I come back, I see how much you're improving."

Ben shook his head, "That's easy to say. But it doesn't really mean anything, because I'm still here dealing with everything."

"Oh no? How do you feel in this exact moment?"

"Not too bad."

"Are you hungry?"

"No."

"Are you too hot or too cold?"

"No."

"Do you have immediate troubles in the next 60 seconds?"

Ben frowned. "I don't think so."

"Then in this moment, you are just fine. It's when you think into the past, or worry about the future, that you begin to feel stressed. Stay in the moment, connect each one to the next, and little by little you'll get to where you want and need to be."

Ben nodded. "But I have so far to go, when I think about everything I've lost."

"You need to stop right there and shift your perspective. Whenever you feel the need to measure where you are, don't use the benchmark of what you used to be. You've got to measure against how far you've come since the accident. That's your new measuring stick."

"All right," nodded Ben. He could see his father was determined to keep him from falling into a negative mindset. "Thanks, Dad."

After considering all the advice he had received from his parents and others, Ben asked certain sentences be written on a piece of paper. He taped that paper to his bedrails, so that he could see it every day.

The only constant in life is change. The past is behind you, the future has yet to come. The only thing you can directly control is the present moment. Enjoy striving to achieve the challenges before you now. Tough times don't last, tough people do.

Ben hoped these important words would help him deal with the many health and other challenges he was dealing with every day. It was the first thing Ben saw when he woke up, and the last thing he saw before he fell asleep. He tried to follow the advice, taking each moment as it came, but one issue in particular was taking its toll. The M.R.S.A. in his leg remained and the treatment for it was causing a new set of health problems.

The only way to treat the severe and deadly M.R.S.A. infection was with Vancomycin intravenously. But the powerful drug was so strong that it put a lot of stress on his veins, causing them to become brittle. Sometimes it took the phlebotomists fifteen minutes or more to find a vein that wouldn't collapse. The longer it would take, the more frustrated they would become and the more painful the end result.

Equally as painful were the frequent moves Ben endured for x-rays and other tests. The process was always tedious and painful. It took four people to transfer him; one for each leg encircled with the heavy Hoffman Devices, and two more to help lift his fragile body.

No matter how careful they were, someone would inevitably jostle his tender legs, which would cause instant and excruciating pain like a powerful bolt of lightning directly through his lower legs. The ride to the x-ray room was always rough. His body amplified every turn or quick stop.

In all, Ben underwent nine surgeries while at Halifax Medical Center. As odd as it sounded, he looked forward to those times. It created a break in the miserable daily routine. The night before the surgery there would be plenty of people in his room, making sure he understood the procedure and was comfortable for the evening. On these nights, his family stayed longer. Though they never said it, he was sure they worried he might not make it. And so they'd spend extra time with him, catching him up on news at home, telling him how much they loved him, and sharing old family stories.

"I remember the first time I met your father," said Doris, putting down the diary she'd been making notes in.

"Yes, it was hate at first sight," laughed Hank.

"Well it wouldn't have been, if you would have brought me a Coke."

"And disobey your parents? I knew who to please if I wanted a tip, so I brought her milk, just as her father asked, which I knew that she hated."

Ben smiled as he listened to them talk about the early days, when Hank had worked as a waiter in the Catskills.

"It was just like that movie that came out a year or two ago," continued Doris, "you know the one, with all the dancing. What was it called Bruce?"

"'Dirty Dancing,' Mom."

"Yes, just like that."

"Except without all the dancing," laughed Hank.

"Yes, but I was a lot younger, in the prime of my day, and I still took up with the hired help," she joked.

"So what happened?" asked Ben. "How did you win her over?"

"Hard work," smiled Doris. "I took his address at the end of summer and we wrote back and forth. I'd never seen a man work so hard to make his dreams come true. He'd gone to school to be an engineer, because that's what his parents wanted, but then turned around and became a teacher after he got his degree. Then he drove a cab at nights and on the weekends and waited tables, just to make sure he could do what he loved. I thought, if a man like that is willing to work that hard to have the life he dreams of, imagine what he would do for his wife and family. So I always knew I made the right choice to marry Dad."

Ben loved hearing stories from his past, sometimes he remembered them, sometimes they seemed brand new. And they always brought the family closer together.

He also looked forward to the few pain free hours after he awoke from surgery. During those times he felt almost normal again. But within three or four hours the intense agony returned with a vengeance. The operated area would feel as if it had caught on fire, while simultaneously being crushed by a semi.

Ben was alone in his room one afternoon when he began feeling unusual chest pains. Comparatively speaking they weren't that bad given everything else he'd been through, just unusual and uncomfortable. He hoped they go away, but by the time the nurse came for his scheduled Hoffman Device cleaning, the pain was still there.

"It's the strangest thing, I've been having these weird pains in my chest," he said casually.

"Oh yeah? Where?" she asked as she prepared the swabs and alcohol.

"In the center of my chest, here," he said motion to a place just above his heart.

She stopped mid-pour and set the bottle of alcohol down. "I'll be right back," she said, hurrying off.

Within seconds a team of doctors and nurses were in Ben's room, poking and prodding him.

"Get that EKG in here stat," ordered a doctor Ben had never seen before.

"Did I hear EKG?" asked Doris appearing in the doorway.

Someone pushed a machine in past her, as the team rushed to hook Ben up.

"Oh no, what's going on? What's going on?" The panic in her voice rose. She pushed through the crowd to grab Ben's hand. "It's all right sweetheart. I'm right here," she assured him. Then turned to the doctor. "Is my son having a heart attack?"

"That's what we're trying to find out," he answered as he watched the monitors being hooked up.

Doris just knew this was the end. The moment she'd feared more than anything else was upon her. Ben was dying right in front of her and there was nothing she could do about it. She squeezed his hand tight to let him know she wasn't going anywhere. She wouldn't leave him no matter how difficult it might be. Tears fell silently down her face as she prayed.

All of a sudden, as the staff had Ben lean forward to attach one last sensor, he let out the loudest, longest burp he'd ever had. It was so long it made *War and Peace* look like the back of a cereal box.

The pain in Ben's chest immediately vanished. "Ok," he smiled brightly, "I'm fine."

"You're fine?" Doris scowled, wiping her eyes. She didn't know whether to smack him or kiss him. "Your heart attack scare nearly gave me a heart attack!"

"I never said I was having a heart attack," Ben reminded everyone.

The nurse, who'd come to clean his wounds, grinned. "I should have known you'd do anything to get out of a cleaning."

Ben laughed at all the stunned faces. It was so funny; it made him laugh harder and harder, which in turn made them laugh. That made him laugh even more, until he became nearly hysterical.

Doris furrowed her brow. "It wasn't that funny."

"Yes it was Mom. You should have seen the look on your face."

"It's still not funny."

He pointed to the slip of paper still posted on his bedrail. "Take Dad's advice and stay in the moment."

"The moment gave me a heart attack."

"Don't you mean you thought it gave me one?"

She gave him a begrudging smile. "Well you certainly do look better than you have in awhile."

"You know what they say," he said still punchy. "Burps and laughter are the best medicine."

Doris shook her head. "Just for that, this one's going in the diary!"

Chapter Fifteen

SCREWED

The medical team that cared for Ben shared a consensus. His injuries and disabilities were permanent. This was his new reality, his new forever. They told him his main priority should be accepting and adapting to his new way of life.

"What scares me most," he confided to Bruce when they were alone, "is that I really don't see a future for someone like me—with all my disabilities."

"So much for following Dad's advice and staying in the moment," joked Bruce.

Ben gave him a dark look. "I'm seriously screwed up and you know it. Dad can say what he likes, but I have to think about these things sometime. I can't stay in the hospital forever. Everyone keeps telling me I need to adjust, but to what?"

Bruce rubbed Ben's shoulder. "It will all work out. You just need to give it some time."

"Time to what? Do you know how scary it is to lie all alone each night and think about these things?"

"Do you remember when we were in high school and everyone was so afraid of that kid on the Westwood team?"

Ben thought for a moment. "You mean that guy that was built like a freight train? What was his name?"

"Mitch."

"And then Coach put you in as a defensive safety in a J.V. game, and you intercepted his play."

Ben smiled. "I thought he was going to kill me."

"But what happened after the game?"

"He said, 'nice interception' when we shook hands."

Bruce nodded. "Sometimes we have such great imaginations that we let them get the better of us. We blow things out of proportion, start to worry, and make things ten times worse than they really are."

"But this is really bad," said Ben, looking down at his legs. "I'm never going to be the same again."

"No, but you can choose what you will be. You can keep your fear from getting out of control and give your time and energy to better things."

Ben supposed that was true, but it wasn't easy. Time seemed to pass so slowly and depression always lurked in the shadows, ready to swoop in and carry him away.

Nights should have been the most restful time for him, but they were worse than the days. His family would seldom stay with him past dinner, because they wanted him to rest and unwind. He felt so alone and lonely when they left.

He tried to watch TV, but he still had problems following a whole program from beginning to end. Then there were the commercials. They were always full of people in their early twenties, smiling and having fun on the beach. They seemed to taunt him, pointing out what he should be doing and what he'd lost. Watching them made him more depressed than ever.

He thought about his new life. What it would be like to be out in the world. He'd never be considered attractive, now with so many scars. How would he manage with his horrible memory and inability to comprehend reading or writing?

He'd had 21 years of good living, maybe that was all he was entitled to. He smiled sadly. He knew he should be grateful; most people didn't get half as much as he'd had. But it was difficult to be grateful when he'd lost so very much. He couldn't help wishing it would have continued forever.

He squeezed Michelle's moon and wished he could escape for a little while, like his family and the hospital staff could. They were always encouraging him to "stay positive" and "never give up," but he couldn't take a break from this existence. They left to their normal lives at the end of the day, while he stayed trapped. Trapped in the hospital, trapped in his bed, trapped in his wreck of a body.

Because of his legs and the heavy devices on them, Ben was stuck on his back, which made it difficult to find a comfortable position to fall asleep. He'd never been able to sleep on his back before, and being in the hospital didn't make it easier. He ached from being immobile, ached from having so much equipment attached to him, and ached from his injuries. Just as he'd begin to dose off, the hospital loudspeakers would blare or someone would drop something.

When he did sleep, it never lasted long. A nurse was always waking him to administer a shot, take a blood sample, or refill his IV. It seemed they always chose the most inopportune times to do it, usually in the middle of a good dream. He'd make his sweet escape and float along finally at peace, only to be slammed back into his body by whatever the nurse was doing in his all-too-real life. He always woke up confused and disoriented, unsure of where he was.

His time in the acute care unit brightened when a friend whose name he recognized called. Suddenly, the phone next to his hospital bed rang.

"Hey bro. It's Jack," he heard other line. "Looks like we'll be graduating together!"

Ben could hardly share his friend's enthusiasm, not with his screwed-up brain. He was feeling especially pessimistic that afternoon and had been playing *what if* again. "Do you ever think about what might have happened if we'd stuck together that night?"

"Sure," said Jack. "I'd be visiting you in jail."

"For what?" asked Ben.

"Your date."

"What date?"

Jack was silent for a moment on the other end of the phone. "Don't you remember what happened earlier that night?"

Ben racked his brain, but most of that night was still a blank.

"We'd picked up these two really hot chicks and made them dinner in our room. They told us they were 19 and things were getting hot and heavy, when my date confessed that your date was sixteen. When I told you, you got really angry, called an end to the night, and kicked both of the ladies out of our room."

"I did?"

"You did. What else could you have done? Your butt would have gone to jail if you slept with her—which was totally where things were headed. Man, you were so pissed. You couldn't believe how easily your life could have been ruined with one misstep. The worst thing was that any guy would have jumped in bed with her in a second. She had a great body and easily looked 21 years old."

Ben was silent, considering the irony.

"Man, I'm sorry," said Jack. "I didn't mean to cock block you…"

"No," Ben cut him off, "it's all right." He started to laugh. "What you're saying is, I was screwed no matter what I did that night."

"I guess you were," laughed Jack.

Chapter Sixteen

THE TRANSFER

At the end of April, after being in the hospital six weeks, doctors announced that Ben would be transferred to a rehabilitation hospital in New York. He was overjoyed. He'd never given much thought to what that meant, but he welcomed the transfer out of acute care. He was sure it would be a big change from his horrible and boring daily routine.

Ben counted down the days. "Only a week to go," he announced to the nurse cleaning his Hoffman Device. "Six days until you're rid of me," he boasted to the orderlies who helped transfer him for tests and x-rays. "Just five days," he said to the woman who brought his lunch.

Four days before the scheduled discharge, Dr. Levinson paid Ben a visit.

"I'm afraid I have some bad news," he said with a grim look.

Ben stared at him, not sure what to expect. Dr. Levinson often had bad news.

"The M.R.S.A. in your leg is still too severe. The rehabilitation hospital isn't equipped to handle it if things get worse. They can't admit you."

Ben's heart fell like a rock. "So what now?"

"You'll be our guest for another week. Then we'll see where we're at."

Ben nodded. "Sure, another week."

"Come now, we can't be all that bad," joked Dr. Levinson. "We've certainly enjoyed having you."

Ben gave him a half smile. He thought about the past six weeks of hell that he had been through. Stuck in the same room, with no visitors, other than his immediate family and his parents' dear friends Karen and Danny, who lived near the Daytona Beach hospital.

The doctor patted Ben's hand. "This is only a minor setback. You should be so proud of how far you've come."

Ben nodded, even though he wanted to cry.

"Do you know that while you were still in a coma I had to go to a three-day conference? I was sure you wouldn't be with us by the time I returned. I was so sure, I even told some of my colleagues. But you were still here when I returned and you had woken up! That's as close to a miracle as I have ever seen."

"So what you're telling me is that you can be wrong?" Ben said glumly.

"No, what I'm telling you is that you have the kind of stamina to handle anything. Your body will fight this infection and you will be out of here in no time. You've waited weeks to be well enough, don't let one or two more get you down."

Ben nodded and lay back on his pillow so that the doctor would leave. It felt as if he was just keeping his head above water and the rehab hospital had been his lifeline. Now it was gone. The darkness he'd been fighting was dragging him under, pulling him to the icy depths of despair. There was no end to being hospitalized.

It wasn't as if he'd healed or his mental disabilities had disappeared, but the transfer did signal a milestone in Ben's life. He was getting better and he no longer needed constant care. He understood that he still had a long way to go. His bones were still shattered, he still wore the Hoffman Devices, his arms were still secured with a brace, and his legs looked like that of a burn survivor, with only the thinly grafted skin over them.

At some level, in his Swiss cheese brain, Ben was sure if he was only allowed out of Halifax Medical Center, that he would be able to start walking again. To him the transfer signaled the beginning of his "real" recovery.

"Sweetheart, what's wrong?" asked Doris breezing into Ben's room.

Ben choked out that his transfer was being delayed. He then told her Dr. Levinson's story about going to the three-day conference.

Doris pursed her lips. "The nerve of that man. He should never have said that to you." she began to pace. "Telling you he thought you'd die…I should go give him a piece of my mind."

"Mom, it's all right. He was just trying to help."

Doris stopped and put her hands on her hips. "Doctors don't help people by telling them they think they're going to die. It was uncalled for."

"But in a strange way it did help, Mom, because if I could prove him wrong once, I can do it again. Maybe I will be healthy and get out of here soon."

* * *

"After I get out of rehab, I still have six weeks of college," Ben said to Lana, the phlebotomist, for the fifth time. "Then I'm going to Seton Hall Law School."

"I thought it was Bridgeport," she gently corrected.

Ben squeezed Michelle's moon as she stuck him. "That's what I meant. Did I tell you this before?"

"Oh, once or twice," she said removing the band from around his arm.

Ben grew red. He was becoming more and more aware that he repeated himself, telling the same stories over and over. To cover his lack of memory, he started beginning his sentences with, "I'm not sure if I said this already..."

He also had many long-term memory issues. There were times he couldn't remember a good friend's name, past vacations, and many things from his childhood. Sometimes he would lie in bed and picture a fraternity brother in his mind. He would then remember a few of the things they did together and parties they drank at. He would then realize that he could not remember the fraternity brother's name. At first, he would rationalize and assume that he forgot friends' names every now and then before the accident. His rationalizations soon turned to fear over how he was going to function in the outside world when he was discharged from the hospital.

When he did remember recent events, it was often difficult to connect the memory with who was involved. He'd remember that he had a phone conversation that morning, but forget that it was with his cousin. Other times, Hank would fly home to New Jersey, and when he'd return, Ben wouldn't remember that he'd been gone at all.

Organizing thoughts was extremely difficult. He understood the concept of taking a trip, but couldn't put the steps together in logical order. When Michelle came to visit, he thought she was checking into a hotel then getting on a plane, then getting a ride to see him, instead of flying, getting a ride, and checking into the hotel.

He tried to stop himself from talking, but it wasn't in his nature to keep quiet. Besides, he'd often forget that he'd made a promise to himself to talk less and listen more.

A week after his first transfer date was cancelled, a second discharge date was also cancelled, and then a third, all due to the M.R.S.A. infection. With each schedule and cancellation, Ben felt as if he were blindfolded on an emotional roller coaster, never knowing when the drops were coming.

When the fourth discharge date was set, Ben refused to feel anything. He'd learned his lesson, like Charlie Brown when Lucy held a football; he wasn't about to be suckered into believing it was really happening. He'd believe it when he saw it.

Part Two

REHABILITATION

Most of the important things in the world have been accomplished by people who have kept on trying when there seemed to be no hope at all.

~ Dale Carnegie, author and motivational speaker

Chapter Seventeen

HOMECOMING

Leaving Halifax Medical Center was like leaving summer camp. On the last morning of Ben's stay, nearly all the doctors, nurses, and staff that had taken care of him stopped by his room to extend their best wishes and say goodbye. Some of the nurses cried, and a few even came in on their days off just to bid farewell.

"In all my years at the hospital, I've never seen someone recover as quickly as your son," Fiona said, hugging Doris.

Doris' eyes misted over. She'd promised herself she wasn't going to cry, but she couldn't help it. "I'm really going to miss you."

"You know where to find us anytime," joked Fiona, reaching up to give Bruce a hug too.

"You really have come such a long way," said Grace, patting Ben's hand.

"Yes, you should be extremely proud of your progress," agreed Dr. Levinson. "Few patients ever accomplish what you have."

"Thank you all for all your help," Ben said as he made his final journey down the long hall out of the ward. He wanted to believe what they were saying, but even if it were true, what did it really matter when he'd lost so much?

"Wait," called Bunny, trailing after them.

"Bunny, you didn't have to come in on your day off," said Doris affectionately.

"I couldn't let my favorite patient go without saying goodbye," she leaned down and hugged Ben. "Be safe and good luck," she said, wiping the tears from her eyes.

Bruce winked at Ben behind Bunny and mouthed, "I told you so."

"Thanks Bunny," said Ben, trying to ignore his brother. They had often speculated that she had a crush on Ben. It was a shame he wouldn't be able to stay longer and find out.

"Oh I almost forgot," she said, reaching in her pocket and withdrawing the slip of paper that had been taped to his bed railing. "You can't leave without this."

Ben reached out and took the crumpled note that had helped him through so many difficult days.

"Thanks again."

Before he could say anything else, the passing scenery distracted him. Being wheeled out of the hospital for the first time in months was scary. It felt like a lifetime since Ben had been outside. He couldn't believe how hot it was when the glass doors of the hospital finally opened. He wondered if prisoners felt similarly when being let of jail after fulfilling years of sentence.

"It's like summer," he said in wonder, taking in large gulps of ocean air.

"It is," agreed his mother, as he was loaded into the ambulance for the short ride to the airport.

Ben had always thought an air ambulance would be some big plane with other patients on it, more like a bus. Perhaps they would show a motivational movie to lift all the passengers' spirits. But he was shocked when they arrived at the local airport. The plane looked smaller than the ambulance he took to get to the airport.

"How are we going to fit in that thing?" he asked Doris.

"Very tightly," she joked, patting his arm.

"It looks like a Cessna."

"I think it is," said Bruce.

"Actually, it's called a turbo jet," said the pilot. "She might be small, but she's got a jet engine." He affectionately patted the side of the tiny tin contraption.

"Sorry we're running behind," greeted the co-pilot, "we had to repair some wing damage."

Bruce's heart nearly jumped into his throat. The thing looked like a flying deathtrap. He was glad he'd be driving Ben's Trans Am home.

"Hi, you must be Bruce, Ben, and Doris" greeted the air nurse. "I'm Mike."

"Can that thing really hold us?" asked Ben.

"Relax kid. You're going to love the in-flight movie," Mike joked.

Bruce hugged Ben and Doris then stepped away from the plane wondering if he would never see either of them again. He watched as they struggled to fit the gurney into the small plane.

Doris climbed in and wedged herself into a corner next to Ben's gurney. She couldn't fully stand up inside the cabin and hated to ask what they did for a bathroom if the need arose.

Ben's ears popped as they took off. The plane felt more like a tin can with wings than an ambulance. He tried not to worry, but the swaying of his gurney made him uneasy. Mike said it was locked down, but what if it broke loose and slammed out the door?

Moments after take-off they hit turbulence. They bumped and knocked about as supplies threatened to jump from their boxes and bins. Each thud jolted Ben more than the last causing him to tense and cry out in pain. He tried squeezing the moon, but it helped little when he never knew when the next bump might hit.

"Try to hang on, we're trying to get out of this as soon as we can," shouted back one of the pilots. "As soon as we have an opportunity to go higher, we will."

"I understand you like football," said Mike to distract Ben. "Who's your favorite player?"

"Wesley Walker," said Ben through gritted teeth.

"The wide receiver with the Jets," smiled Mike. "Why him?"

"He's legally blind in one eye. It's amazing that he can get to the pros with a disability like that."

"Gives you something to look forward to?"

"Me? No, I never wanted to go pro. I just admire him for overcoming the odds. He's always been my favorite."

Doris nodded. "Ben always roots for the underdog."

"No kidding? Who else do you follow?"

"I love Kareem Abdul-Jabbar."

"That cat's no underdog, why him?"

"The dude's in his 40s and still competes with the young pros. That's awesome."

The rest of the seven-hour flight was consumed with sports talk. Though Ben couldn't completely forget the pain, Mike's cheerful conversation was enough to distract him. By the time they landed, it was already dark.

"It's warm here too," marveled Ben as he was wheeled into another ambulance for the final leg of his trip. He took in the sights and sounds of the outdoors, knowing they would be his last for a long time.

Ben's new home, Helen Hayes Rehabilitation Hospital, was in West Haverstraw, New York. He was anxious to get there after being cooped up in such confined spaces all day. But suddenly the ambulance pulled over.

"What's going on?" asked Doris.

"Accident," said one of the EMT's.

"Is it bad?" she asked craning her neck to see through the windshield.

"That's what we're going to find out. Since this is a non-emergency transport, we're obligated to stop and offer our assistance," he explained before leaving.

"You see that Ben?" Doris asked still watching the accident scene ahead. "There are people worse off than you in this world."

Something in Ben shifted when she said that. He stopped to realize how far he really had come in such a short time. He'd almost died, twice. They'd thought he might be a vegetable and here he was talking. Now he was going to rehab and in a few weeks he'd be using his arms and hopefully walking again one day.

Though he couldn't see what was going on outside, he prayed that whomever was hurt wasn't as bad off as he had been. And if they were, that they would have as much support as he had. Crazy as it sounded, he finally was beginning to realize how lucky he truly was.

Chapter Eighteen

SECOND LIFE

West Haverstraw, New York, May

In many ways Ben's second life began with his arrival at Helen Hayes Rehabilitation Hospital. It was there that he planned to reclaim much of himself. He was looking forward to re-learning so many things that he had taken for granted previously. Though the doctors said otherwise, he knew he would walk and maybe even run again one day.

Hank greeted the ambulance when it pulled up.

"There's my guy," he said as the ambulance doors opened.

"Hey Dad," Ben said, happy to see a familiar face. He was exhausted, but somehow knowing both his parents would be with him made everything seem better. Because it was the weekend, things were quiet and slow at the rehabilitation hospital.

At Halifax, Ben had his own private room due to the M.R.S.A. infection. But at Helen Hayes, he was no longer a risk to other patients and so he was admitted to a four-person room, while Hank and Doris took care of the final paperwork.

"Now because you're traumatic brain injury patient, you'll be on our neurological floor," explained the nurse who was helping Ben settle in.

Ben shook his head. "There must be a mistake. I'm supposed to go to rehab so I can walk again."

The nurse smiled, "And you will, but because you have a traumatic brain injury, hospital regulations require you to stay in this unit for the peace, quiet, and safety of other patients." The nurse matter-of-factly

83

tucked the covers around him as she spoke. "There now, be sure to call me if you need anything," she said brightly.

Ben nodded vaguely. All he'd heard was "for the peace, quiet, and safety of other patients." Did they think he might endanger those around him? His heart skipped a beat. He'd never hurt anyone in his life...at least he was pretty sure he hadn't. Why were they treating him like a criminal? Was there something more they weren't telling him?

His cheeks burned. As if his injuries were bad enough, now the hospital staff didn't trust him. Tears welled in his eyes. He'd become a gruesome freak of nature.

Ben had assumed that he would be in a room with other guys in their 20s, who were in bad car or motorcycle accidents.

But instead of young accident survivors like himself, his roommates were elderly stroke patients in their 80s and 90s. None were lucid and all had severe mental impairments. Ben could understand why they might keep his roommates locked away. They were in their own worlds, communicating with no one, mumbling, and screaming at random. One kept repeatedly throwing up, while the others stank from soiling themselves and had to be changed like infants. It made sense to keep an eye on them, but he wasn't one of them. Yet there he was, more alone than ever stuck among the broken old men.

"Good to have you home, Ben," said Hank as he left.

Home? Thought Ben. This was nothing like home. This was a never-ending nightmare. How had he fallen so far? He'd been healthy and popular in college, with everything to look forward to. Now he was stuck with three shells of men waiting to die. The life he'd known and any happiness he'd had were things of the past. There was no reason to continue. His life was over. The more he thought, the worse he felt.

CHAPTER NINETEEN

ARTEMIS & DR. HUGHES

"A re you ready for your big day tomorrow?" asked a huge therapist, who looked more like a linebacker.

"Can't wait," grinned Ben.

"Oh, you won't be saying that by the afternoon," joked the massive man.

"Are you kidding? I might just jog all the way to New York City once they let me out of bed."

"Now that's an attitude I haven't seen in awhile."

"I expect you haven't seen too many people like me in awhile either," said Ben, tilting his head towards his aging roommates. One was asleep, while another was carrying on a conversation with someone who wasn't there, and the third appeared to be reading an upside-down book.

"You can say that again. Name's Artemis," said the man, extending a large paw of a hand, "but most folks around here just call me Art."

"Nice to have a name for the face. Though I have to warn you, my mind's not so good these days. You'll probably have to remind me of your name every now and then."

"No worries big guy. I got you covered."

It struck Ben as funny that such a huge guy would be calling him "big guy," especially since he'd wasted away since the accident.

"Do you know what they're going to do with me tomorrow?"

"You'll find out soon enough for yourself. All I can say is that we will work you so hard, you'll be yearning for the good ole days when all you had to do was sit and rot in bed."

"No, not me, the moment these Hoffman Devices come off, I'll be running several miles every day. It will be one of those great moments in sporting history, you'll see. I'll prove everyone wrong. I'm going to be the first of my kind."

Art chuckled. "I hope for your sake that you're right. But a little advice, remember what you're saying now when you feel the burn and channel all enthusiasm into dogmatism. Do that and you'll be all right."

Ben frowned. "What's that supposed to mean?"

Art saluted Ben. "I'd like to stay but duty calls," he said, disappearing out the door.

Ben didn't have long to wait for his answer. The next day he met with his orthopedic team. Along with his fresh start, he'd made the decision to have all doctors deliver medical information to him first, as opposed to his father. He not only wanted to feel more independent, but he was sick of hearing second hand and heavily edited versions of his condition and prognosis from his parents.

From then on the doctors had to follow his wishes concerning treatment and prognosis. He was so ready to get the heavy devices off his legs, he could almost taste it.

"Good afternoon," said a thin, tall man, trailed by several residents in a perfect line. He had thin, curly hair and metal rim glasses. He reminded Ben of an accountant more than an orthopedic surgeon.

"I'm Dr. Hughes."

Ben shook his hand, "So, when can I walk?"

"I'm afraid we won't know for awhile."

"What do you mean?"

The doctor took out a little notepad and drew sketches of Ben's legs. As he drew he explained, "Being that your fractures were so serious, coupled with the infection, your leg bones have not yet begun to heal."

Ben shook his head. "How can that be? It's been two months! Bones heal, they have to!"

"Under average conditions they would, but as I said, your injuries are quite severe. Your body has used all its energy to fight the infection, instead of mending the broken bones. It's what we call a complete non-union. It means that even though the Hoffman Devices are holding your bones in place, the separations between the bones have not fused back together."

"But they will heal eventually, right?"

"That is my hope, however to help get you there, you will need to undergo three or four more surgeries."

Ben fell back onto his pillows. Not more surgery. The constant pain was becoming more manageable and he was just starting to feel some improvement. He blew out a long breath. "How will these surgeries help?"

"Our goal is to help you walk again. In order to do that, you need to be able to put weight on your legs. Therefore, the first surgery will be to remove the Hoffman Devices. Then, within a day or two we will perform a second surgery to fit you with a similar but smaller device, which we believe will be better suited to your injuries. The next surgery will be to insert a metal rod into your right leg to help stabilize the bone for about a year. When that year is through, your bone should be a complete union, and we will schedule a fourth surgery to remove the rod."

As Dr. Hughes spoke, water welled in Ben's eyes and spilled down his cheeks. He'd thought with all his cognitive and mental disabilities, at least he could look forward to being able to walk again. But now even that seemed like a pipe dream.

The only good news that came out of the meeting with his team was that he was being transferred off the neurological floor and into a private room in the orthopedic ward due to his long-standing infection and risk of reoccurrence.

It seemed Ben was always in pre-op or post-op. He felt more than ever that he had become a human pincushion. His parents supportively attended every one of his surgeries waiting for hours on end to hear the outcome. He was glad they were so close by, but it did little to numb the pain.

Ben didn't have the luxury of enjoying a few hours of pain-free bliss after his bone surgeries that he had had after the surgeries he had in Florida. All his significant Florida bone surgeries had taken place while he was in a coma. The soft-tissue surgeries had been bad enough, with anesthesia masking the pain for a few hours after. But bones surgeries were different. They involved bone manipulation, repositioning, cutting, drilling and inserting screws. The pain from the bone surgeries were the likes of which he'd never felt before.

He'd thought he'd tasted everything the surgery candy shop had to dish out, but he hadn't even come close. The only thing that worked on torture of such magnitude was the pain killer Demerol. The effects of the painkiller were swift and total. But as welcome as it was, it never lasted long.

Ben hated having visitors after the surgeries. He always felt like he had to put on a show for them, to try to convince them that he was normal and okay. It was better than letting them worry or all the questions and guilt he would get if he didn't do his dog and pony show. Having visitors after a surgery left him both physically and mentally drained. When that happened, depression consumed him.

How could he stay in the moment when his moments were so rotten? He felt miserable and very weak. He didn't even have the strength to kill himself if he wanted to.

He knew it was a morbid thought, but it was the truth. Whenever he thought about the past, he became more miserable. It was such a depressing escape from his muddled brain and broken body.

* * *

"Is there something going on that I don't know about?" Ben asked his parents when they came to visit.

"Like what?" his mother asked.

"I don't know, some big event or maybe a school trip or something?"

Doris furrowed her brow. "I don't think so."

"That's strange."

"What is?" asked Hank.

"I don't think any of my friends have come to visit since I got here."

Doris and Hank exchanged glances. Ben looked from one to the other.

"They haven't, have they? Or did I forget?"

"You didn't forget," said Doris, patting his hand. "Your father asked them to stay away…"

"What? Dad, is that true?" Ben demanded.

"Calm down, Ben, it's in your best interest," said Hank quietly.

"Since when is keeping my friends from me in my best interest?"

"I told them to give you a little time to adjust to your new accommodations."

"Adjust! My goal isn't to adjust, it to get out of here as quickly as possible. Having friends come to see me will help me do that much quicker!"

"There's no need to raise your voice."

"I will raise my voice if I feel like it, especially if I'm being, being... un, under...if I think people are going behind my back!"

"You're father is just trying to help."

"Stay out of this, Mom."

Hank crossed his arms. "You don't know what you're saying. You're getting worked up over nothing."

"I'm not crazy and I know exactly what I'm saying. How dare you tell my friends to stay away."

"It was a logical decision..."

"Do you have any idea what my life is like? Do you have any idea what it's like to be trapped in your body? To feel constant pain? To be surrounded by people four times your age who smell like death? And to be bored silly on top of it, knowing there's not a thing you can do to escape any of it?

"Everyone keeps telling me I have so much to live for, but if this is all my life is, then I'd be crazy not to question why I'm trying. Because this," he pointed around his room, "isn't worth it. Can't you see I need hope, I need joy, I need my friends? They are my motivation to get out of here," Ben said with blazing eyes. "I don't need anyone deciding for me who I can and can't see. From now on, I make the decisions about who comes to visit."

CHAPTER TWENTY

OLD FRIENDS

"Hey you," Cassandra, Ben's longtime steady girlfriend, greeted him.

It felt like ages since he'd seen her last. She was even more beautiful than he remembered with her long dark hair and big green eyes. She had a smile that could light up a room. He touched his left eye, feeling the ugly scar that had formed over it. His heart was beating a million miles a minute. What would she think of him now that he was no longer a well-built athlete and an honor roll student?

They'd started dating in high school when he was a senior and she was a junior. When it came time for college, they didn't want to be like all those couples that attend their boyfriend or girlfriend's university just to "stay together." Instead he'd gone to Trenton State and she'd gone to nearby Rutgers University. They'd called each other every night and spent most Saturdays together.

Throughout college they'd had an understanding that they could date other people, if they wanted to. They'd both tested that rule a couple of times, but for the most part, they preferred each other's company.

"Where've you been?" he joked as she came around the bed to hug him. He awkwardly raised his arms to encircle her.

"I thought I'd lost you," she cried into his shoulder.

"No, can't get rid of me that easy." He sunk into her warmth. She always smelled so good. *Anais, Anais,* the name of her perfume, popped into his head. After months of sterile hospital surroundings and the aroma of alcohol and medicine, not to mention being repeatedly pinched, poked, and prodded, it felt good to relax in her embrace. He closed his eyes and let her scent carry him back to the good old days.

"Don't you ever, ever, do that to me again," she said pulling back to get a good look at him.

Ben went pink under her penetrating gaze. "I'll try not to."

"You better not, we have things to do. Restaurants to eat at. Places to visit."

Ben laughed. It was like old times with her planning their social calendar.

Cassandra gently touched Ben's cheek. "It's so good to have you back."

It was the first time since the accident Ben felt really felt good again. The feeling continued long after Cassandra went home. But it didn't matter because things were finally on track. He had his girlfriend back, and he had a new medical team who shared his goal of getting him out of the hospital. Then one day soon, he and Cassandra would get married and start a family.

His lips twitched in amusement. Maybe the accident had screwed him up worse than he thought. Cassandra was always the one who talked about getting married, while he avoided the subject.

No sooner had Cassandra left when several of Ben's fraternity brothers showed up.

"Hey guys," he greeted them, trying to sit up a little straighter in bed, so that he would appear stronger. As he shifted his weight, the corner of Michelle's moon worked its way out from under the covers. Ben nonchalantly pushed it under the blankets with his elbow.

"I knew I couldn't trust you with my shirt," joked Ace.

"What?" asked Ben.

"You know the shirt you borrowed the night of the accident."

"I did? You let me wear one?"

"Only the white V-neck with the brown stripes."

"Oh man, that shirt was totally awesome. I'm so sorry."

"Forget about it. We're just glad you're okay," said Ace, playfully punching Ben in the shoulder.

Ben tried not to wince. He was glad his brothers had come to see him and yet, he was completely embarrassed. He wanted them to remember him as a muscular, confident, intelligent guy, and not the disabled, senile, old man he'd become. He was also concerned that they would report back to his other friends at school that he wasn't the same guy he was before the accident.

"So how're they treating you?" asked Jake.

"It's like the Ritz in here. You should all give it a try."

"So," Jake said, rocking back and forth on his feet, "What've you been up to lately?"

"Geezes Jake, what do you think he's been up to?" asked Patrick.

Ace rolled his eyes. "When do you start physical therapy?"

"Soon, I hope. Tell me what you guys have been doing."

"You know, the usual. Working on my car, going to the shore, hanging out at the club..." Jake' voice drifted off, embarrassed to be doing so much, when Ben couldn't.

After a little while, Patrick cleared his throat, "You know we probably oughta get going, there's that thing."

"What thing?" asked Ace.

Patrick gave him a meaningful look. "That thing we promised to do this evening."

"Oh, that's right. Our thing," Ace said unconvincingly. "You coming?" he asked Jack as they said their goodbyes.

"No, I think I'll hang here for awhile longer," Jack answered as the brothers headed out.

Jack was the only brother Ben didn't mind coming to visit. They'd been best friends ever since Jack chose him as his "big brother" three years ago. He'd been with him from the beginning and seen him in the coma. So Ben knew Jack appreciated just how far he'd come, even if he sounded like a crazy old man sometimes.

Chapter Twenty-One

BREAK THROUGH

"Why so down?" asked a familiar, deep voice one afternoon. Ben looked up from his revelry. "Art! What are you doing here?"

"They shuffle us around whenever they're short staffed. So what's going on? Where's that go get 'em attitude of yours?"

Ben shook his head. "Have you ever felt all alone?"

"Sure, you can't look like me and blend into a crowd."

"That's just it. It's like I don't belong anywhere now. My friends come to see me, but I'm not really one of them anymore. I look at the other patients here, and don't feel like one of them either."

"Do you like basketball?"

"Sure."

"Then maybe you should go down and check out the wheelchair basketball court. You might make some new friends there."

Ben frowned, "I don't know. If I get too comfortable here, I might stop trying. Then I'll never get out of here."

"Never's a mighty long time. Bet that pretty girlfriend of yours would have something to say about that."

Ben turned his head into his pillow. Lately he'd been wondering how fair it was to keep Cassandra hanging on to someone like him. "I don't know how long I can do this," he whispered to Art.

"As my old football coach used to say, 'You can do it as long as it takes.'"

"You played football?"

"Double A state champs in '80 and '81."

"I played ball too," said Ben, thinking back to how effortlessly he'd run up and down the field doing those crazy striders the coach made them do. "We were nowhere near as good as that, but we had an awesome coach."

"Oh yeah? What was he like?"

"He was a little Italian guy, former Marine, maybe five feet, six inches, but he was a force to be reckoned with. No one crossed Coach Mainieri."

"Oh, mean guy?"

"No, no, tough, but we all respected him. In fact, I couldn't stand the idea of not living up to his expectations. I always wanted to please him. He changed my life."

"How so?"

"What I learned from him was that we could achieve anything we wanted to on the football field, if we were willing to pay the price to get there. Coach's rule was that whenever our minds and bodies were tired and told us to slow down; we should use that message as a trigger to work twice as hard for as long as possible. If we did that, he guaranteed we'd improve on the field. If we applied that formula off the football field as well, then we could accomplish anything."

Ben stopped short, thinking about what the coach had instilled in him. It still applied all these years later. He knew it applied because he'd used that rule over and over in his life.

Coach Mainieri was famous for his striders. He'd make the entire team run 50 yards down the field, then turn around and race back, and then repeat it once more before resting momentarily for the next set of striders. The goal was to be first. Ben was almost always second to last, which meant that he was the second slowest runner on the team.

It was embarrassing to be known for being so slow. So Ben considered what he learned from the coach and made it his mission to become one of the fastest on the team. He'd get up early, just so he could go work on his running. He'd run after school and on weekends. He'd never been more committed to anything in his life. He poured his heart and soul into running faster. When he felt like slowing down, he used it as a catalyst to run twice as hard for as long as possible.

In time, he worked his way up to the middle of the pack during the Coach's striders, then to the front of the group. By the end of the season he was regularly one of the first few to complete the exercise.

Ben trusted that the formula could be applied to anything in life. Ben had always been a below average student. He'd always assumed he was just not good at schoolwork. Never mind the fact that he stuffed assignments in his pants' pocket instead of organizing them neatly in a folder or sometimes forgot to do his homework all together.

He wondered if old Mainieri just might be right. Maybe he could become "smarter" if he applied the rule to his studies. And so he gave it a try. When he had the urge to put a school book down, he'd used that as a reason to study twice as hard for as long as possible. When he wanted to quit, he'd remember his football running success and push on.

In a single semester, he went from being a C and D student to being on the honor roll. It would be a wonderful feeling to be recognized for being one of the "smart kids" one day. When it came time for college he'd applied the very same rule. It had not only sustained him, it helped him consistently keep at least a 3.65/4.00 grade point average throughout college. He'd become president of the college's Blue Key Honor Society, Economics Honors Society, as well as several honor organizations and clubs.

Ben had always felt like he was getting something over on everybody, because his high grades weren't from being "academically smart" – they were simply a result of putting more effort into his studies than his peers.

Such victories had convinced him that anybody can be the top student in their class, a great musician, athlete, teacher, chef, doctor, lawyer, or anything else for that matter, if when they start to feel tired, they push themselves twice as hard for as long as possible.

He looked at the slip of paper taped to his hospital bed and something clicked inside him. When he wanted to give up, giving something his complete focus and pushing himself as hard as he could for as long as possible was exactly what he needed to do in his recovery! It wasn't just words or a half-dead coping mechanism, it worked in real life! He knew from experience that it worked. He'd just forgotten the rule!

CHAPTER TWENTY-TWO

PHYSICAL THERAPY

Despite the prognosis of his doctors, Ben still wanted to fulfill his life's dreams. He was determined to walk, and even go back to running and weightlifting every day. He wanted to graduate college with high honors, go to law school, pass the bar exam, and become an attorney. He also wanted to get married and have a bunch of kids.

In order to do those things, he would have to quit feeling sorry for himself and follow Coach Mainieri's rule. Each time he felt like giving up, he would work twice as hard for as long as possible. If it took him a year, two years, or even five to get better, he would do it. He just had to remind himself to never give up.

By mid-May, the surgeries were behind Ben and he was well on his way to recovery. He now had a smaller lighter device on his left leg, which extended from his knee to his ankle. It reminded him of a vertical towel bar, though he had to admit it made it much easier to move his leg. Though he was still stuck in unfashionable hospital gowns, he envisioned that he might be able to wear pants over the new appliance.

His right leg was completely free of external devices. Dr. Hughes explained that the titanium bar that he'd inserted into Ben's leg made him like a super hero of sorts. It was so strong that it could bear the weight of his body so that he could begin walking again.

Ben was surprised when he met Colleen, another one of his physical therapists. She was a petite woman in her late twenties with long, brown hair. She looked more like a nymph than the big, burly man he had envisioned hauling him to his feet and teaching him to walk again. But looks can be deceiving. Colleen was just as strong as his male therapists. Best of all, she seemed just as eager as Ben was to help him get back on his feet.

"Ready to get this party started?" she asked on her first visit to his room.

"Take me away," Ben replied enthusiastically.

"Actually, the first lesson starts right here," she corrected him.

"In my room?" he asked skeptically.

"Yep, right there in your bed. Before you can get to physical therapy, you need to know how to transfer yourself to a wheelchair."

Ben had always assumed someone would come get him. He thought maybe they'd prop him up and he'd just start walking in some safe place maybe with bars to hold on to and a few mats on the floor.

"Since your arms are stronger than your legs right now, I want you to use them to shift your weight." She sat down on the bed next to him. "I want you to put them down next to your hips like this," she shifted her own weight and lifted herself up.

It reminded Ben of something little kids might do fooling around in the yard. Look at me! I'm walking on my hands! But when he tried the move it was a lot more difficult than he remembered. He hadn't just lost weight since the accident; he'd lost a lot of muscle. Not to mention he was still wearing the brace for his fractured clavicle. He finally managed a sloppy half move, that got him to the edge of the bed.

"Way to go," Colleen smiled. She looked at her watch. "Our hour's almost up. You've done really well for your first day."

Sweat poured down Ben's back and his arms burned from the hard work, but Coach Mainieri's rule echoed in his head. When your mind tells you it's time to quit, use that message as a trigger to work twice as hard for as long as possible.

"But we still have a few more minutes; right?" Ben asked panting. "Let's keep going. What do I do next?"

She frowned. "I don't want you over doing it on your first day. You'll be sore by tomorrow and then you may not want to work."

He shook his head. "No, not me. I can take it. What's next?"

"You do realize we won't be able to finish today."

"I know, but I still want to learn."

"All right, I suppose it wouldn't hurt." She sat back down on the bed and demonstrated the method for transferring from the bed to a wheelchair. "Always make sure the chair is locked before you try this or it could slip out from under you."

Ben nodded, watching her intently. He basically needed to use his upper body to guide his butt into wheelchair and then drag his legs with him. But when he tried it himself, he couldn't come close. He just didn't have the strength or coordination.

"Okay, time's really up now." Colleen patted his back. "Great session. You keep going like this and I will have you walking in no time. See you same time tomorrow."

"Wait," called Ben as she pushed the wheelchair out of the room. "Can you leave that behind? I want to practice some more."

She smiled. "You really are determined aren't you? I'm sorry, but we can't let you work unsupervised, hospital regulations."

"Then stay and work with me. I can go at least another hour."

Colleen laughed. "I'm sure you could, but I can't. I have other patients to see. Besides, most insurance companies only allow us to work with patients for one hour a day. I'm sorry, but that's all they will cover."

"That's all right," Ben said, trying to hide his disappointment. "See you tomorrow."

CHAPTER TWENTY-THREE

SHOES!

Since Ben couldn't physically continue his therapy for more than an hour, he visualized what he needed to do, going over and over the steps in his mind. Each time he took himself through the process, he tried to imagine what each part of his body felt like and what it should be doing to accomplish the task of sliding into that wheelchair. He thought about it so much that the memories of what he should be doing seemed to imprint on his muscles.

Within a week, thanks to the help of Colleen and the other therapists, he was able to successfully transfer from his bed to his wheelchair. As soon as he could do the independent transfer, he was given permission to roam the hallways of Helen Hayes. He felt light and alive again. He loved being in control of his own mobility and feeling the wind rush over his face as he sped through the corridors. In reality, he knew he probably wasn't going all that fast, but to him it felt like the Indy 500. It was the most free-spirited feeling he'd ever had. As soon as the thought popped into his head, he laughed. It was amazing how he appreciated the smallest things, since he had nearly lost everything.

Ben wheeled himself to the basketball court. He figured it couldn't hurt to play a few games. At the very least it might help him get his strength back. Several people were on the court when he arrived. Everyone playing was on a wheelchair. A few were dribbling balls, while others were doing more talking than warming up.

The whistle blew and two guys wheeled their way to center court for the face off. Just like regular basketball, they were playing shirts and skins. Skins got the ball and they headed down the court, chairs squeaking as metal locked with metal.

"Pathetic," said a guy rolling up next to Ben to watch the game.

"I thought they were kind of good," said Ben, marveling at how easy they made it look to race down the court while dribbling.

"If you're into that sort of thing."

Ben turned to get a good look at him. The guy was a couple years older than him, with spiked, black hair and fierce dark eyes. "Is there something wrong with what they're doing?"

His companion snorted, "They're a bunch of losers."

Ben frowned. "Why do you say that?"

"Just look at them, they've given up. They don't even want to walk anymore."

"Maybe they can't or maybe it's too soon. Besides, it doesn't look like you're walking either."

"I would be if the doctor hadn't messed up my last surgery."

"Don't listen to Duane," said a beautiful blonde wheeling up on the other side of Ben. "He's a bitter, bitter man."

"Because they're all in a conspiracy to keep us here," growled Duane.

The blonde waved him off. "Isn't it time for your medication or something?"

"Wouldn't you just like it if I ate some more of their poison? They're probably paying you to remind me."

"You wish."

Duane turned back to Ben, "The longer we stay in these things, the more this place gets paid to take care of us. They don't want us to get better. Think about it," he said, tapping his head as he rolled out of the gym.

"Sorry about Duane," said the blonde. "He's a little touched in the head."

Ben nodded, suddenly feeling self-conscious about his own brain injury.

"My name's Eve, what's yours?"

"Ben."

"So are you going to play?" she asked, nodding her head towards the court.

"Oh I don't think so."

"Why not? I bet you'd be good."

"All right," he said, wanting to impress her. "I'll play if you do too."

She laughed. "Sorry, I can't. I'm paralyzed from the chest down. It takes all my strength just to move this chair."

Ben was having a hard time not staring at her. She was absolutely gorgeous. "May I ask what happened to you?"

Eve shrugged. "There's not a lot to tell. I used to be a model, but my boyfriend was terribly jealous of all the people I met at work. One night we had a huge fight. I was so angry I stormed out. I got in my car just to get away and tore off down the highway. I was so upset I couldn't even see straight. I must have hit the gas pretty hard. Because the next thing I knew, my car was flipping over. I don't remember too much about it, but they say it rolled several times. When I woke up, I was like this."

"I don't remember much of my accident either," nodded Ben. "Tell me, is everyone around here as negative as Duane?"

"Are you kidding?" laughed Eve, "most people are worse."

Eve became one of Ben's best friends at Helen Hayes. Though she was joking about the other patients' attitudes, she was right. Ben had a difficult time hanging out with many of them because he always felt worse when he was done talking with them. It seemed like none of them could move beyond their pasts to help themselves in the present. They were often angry or worse yet, so sad that it was difficult to spend time with them.

Whenever he could, Ben wheeled outside and sat by the front entrance to the hospital. He could just make out the distant mountains' changing shades of blue on the horizon. While he had always enjoyed visiting the ocean, he loved the mountains. The beautiful mountains meant he was home. It gave him great peace to know he was growing stronger in their shadow.

"Hi there," he greeted a couple on their way into the hospital.

They nodded and smiled.

"Beautiful day," he said to an elderly lady as she followed the others in.

"Yes it is," she smiled.

Ben made a special effort to greet everyone who passed through the hospital doors. He looked at it as therapy. Not only did it give him a chance to practice speaking, but it was always an adventure because he never knew whom he would meet or who might stop and talk to him.

Of course, most people just smiled and went about their business. It didn't occur to him until several days later that most people probably thought he was just some crazy guy who didn't know what was going on.

The thought struck him as funny, until he began to laugh as if he were one of those "crazy guys."

In the coming days, Ben had plenty to smile about. Dr. Hughes gave him the green light to begin putting weight on his legs. Walking was no longer a far-off fantasy; it was an obtainable, real goal and Ben was determined he would make it happen.

"I have something for you," said Hank when he came to visit on the afternoon that Ben got the news.

"What is it?" Ben asked, looking at the large, brown paper bag his father was holding.

"Take a look," Hank said setting the bag in front of him.

Ben opened the bag and laughed. "My old high tops!" It had been more than four months since he had worn shoes. But he couldn't remember why his dad would have them. "Wow, where'd you find them?"

"They were in your closet."

"I knew that," Ben said, trying to cover. As he sat looking at the shoes a vague memory of putting them away after a pick-up game of basketball the summer before crept into his head. He wondered if it had really happened or if it just seemed to make sense.

"Isn't it time for therapy?" asked Hank, taking the handles of Ben's wheelchair.

"It's all right Dad, I've got it," said Ben, taking off at a good pace. Hank had to chase after him down the short hall to the physical therapy room.

"Look what I have," Ben said, proudly holding up one of his battered, white, high tops for Colleen to see. "I'm going to wear shoes like a civilized person."

"Well it's about time," she joked. "Here let me help you," she said bending down to put the shoes on his feet.

"Aren't you breaking one of your own rules?" Ben asked as he watched her.

"What rule would that be?"

"I just thought you'd make putting on my shoes part of my therapy."

"Maybe later, but it takes some fine motor skills to lace these babies up and we're working on walking today."

Tears came to Hank's eyes as he watched his son and the therapist happily chatting. Just a few short months ago he was told Ben probably wouldn't make it, now here he was learning to walk again.

"What's the matter, Dad?" Ben asked, catching his father wiping a tear away.

"I've dreamed so long that this moment would come, and now it's here," Hank dabbed at his eyes with a handkerchief.

"Okay, Ben," said Colleen drawing his attention back to the task at hand. "This is a harness for extra support as you work out," she said attaching a length of leather around his waist.

"Pretty fashionable," he joked, eager to get walking.

"And these are your parallel bars. You're going to place a hand on each one of them, just like the bed transfer and stand between them. Let's go ahead and give it a try, just to see where we are."

Ben gave a giant heave, but nothing happened. He was still dragging his legs into the wheelchair, but somehow he'd thought standing would be different. Now that he was trying to put weight on them, they felt like jelly and much too weak to support his body.

"Come on, you can do it," Colleen encouraged, holding on to his belt to help ease him up.

Ben swayed as he tried to stand. Blood rushed through his veins down his legs. It tickled and prickled similar to a body "falling asleep," only this was much worse. Feeling the blood flowing into his lower legs wasn't invigorating; rather, it was both weird and very painful. On top of that, his brain injury had messed up his sense of balance. Exhausted, he collapsed back into his seat.

Walking was going to be a lot more difficult than he had imagined. The road ahead was still much longer than he had thought. Over the next four days, he worked very hard on standing independently off his wheelchair. No wonder it takes a baby a whole year to learn to walk, he thought. He'd always taken the action for granted, and now he was learning just how really complicated standing and walking really were. As the days went by, he marveled at the intricacy of it all. Though he wished his injuries on no one, he thought it would be a great lesson for people to understand the complexities of walking and realize how lucky they are to be able to do so.

On the fifth day of learning to walk, Ben wheeled down to physical therapy determined that this would be the day. He took his harness from the hook on the wall and was fumbling with the buckle by the time Colleen joined him.

"Come on, what are you waiting for slow poke? We've got work to do," he greeted her.

"Slow poke?" she said, checking her watch, "I've still got three minutes."

"Well then, I'll just have to start without you," he said wheeling to the parallel bars.

"I'm coming, I'm coming. Can't you give a girl a break?"

"Not today. I'm going to do it."

"All right, give it your best shot," she said, taking up her post.

Slowly he eased himself into position. Inch by inch he pulled himself up, just as he envisioned every night. At first it was more of a right angle. Had he been more limber, he could have put his hands down and done a straight leg crawl. Then he worked his way up to a hunch like an old man. Finally, little by little, he fully uncurled until he stood straight. He'd forgotten how different things looked while standing. He took one hand off the bar and then the other until he was balancing fully under his own power. He never felt taller.

"Look, look at me! I'm really doing it!" Of course he'd said he would, but only half believed it until that moment. "I'm standing. I'm really standing!"

"You're a regular Carl Lewis." Colleen clapped.

"How long do you think I can do it for?"

"Let's go for a minute," she said timing him.

"You're on!"

As the seconds ticked by, he'd never realized how long a minute could be. He breathed heavily, blowing out air as Colleen gave the countdown. "Five, four, three, two..."

He collapsed into his chair just as she said one. He'd done it. "I've got to go call my parents!" He said wheeling for the door.

"Wait, what about the rest of your session?"

He spun the chair around, "Even Carl Lewis takes a break once in awhile."

Chapter Twenty-Four

THERE ARE NO QUICK FIXES, ONLY HARD WORK

B en spent the rest of the day calling friends and family to boast of his great accomplishment.

The next morning he woke up with all of his leg muscles feeling painfully sore. It reminded him of how he felt the morning after his first high school football practice. But he welcomed this kind of pain. Any time his muscles hurt, that was a sign that they were getting stronger. He had a momentary flashback visualizing his high school football team exclaiming, "No pain, no gain!"

"There's my slacker," joked Colleen the next afternoon when Ben joined her.

"What can I say? That's me," he grinned. "What's next coach, the quarter mile or maybe a half marathon?"

"How about we start with a step?"

"One small step for Ben, one giant leap for mankind," he said, getting into position. Though he still ached like crazy from the day before, he wasn't going to let anything stand in his way.

Ben stood just as he did the day before, but then something inside him froze when Colleen asked him to put one foot forward. No matter how much he wanted to, he just couldn't bring himself to do it. It was partly because his body was still so weak. His head injury was forcing him to use other parts of his brain to accomplish the same tasks. But mostly it was fear, plain and simple. He felt that if he put his foot forward, the corresponding movement of the rest of his body would defy logic. It didn't seem humanly possible.

"We don't realize how lucky we are to be able to walk. It's not at all easy. Good thing we learn to walk as babies." Ben told Jack, the next time he came to visit.

Jack shook his head. "I don't know how you do it, man. I always looked up to you, but now you're really my hero."

"Yeah, that's exactly what I was trying to do. All this," he gestured to his legs, "was in hopes of becoming your hero."

"Smart ass."

"I'm telling you learning to walk again is really scary. What if I fall? It would be humiliating. And my therapist is so petite. What if I land on her and squash her?"

"You always did have a way with the ladies. Maybe you could make falling one of the hundred ways to pick up a chick. Is she cute?"

"She's very pretty. I think I'm falling in love."

"Really? Do you think it's mutual?"

"Oh she likes me well enough, but I'm just a patient to her."

"Too bad, older women can be really hot."

"Down boy, she's my therapist," laughed Ben.

"Makes me want to have a little therapy of my own. When's your next session?"

Ben shook his head. "Very funny. Besides, I'm sure Cassandra would have plenty to say about it."

"So what are you going to do?"

"I'm here to learn how to walk again, so that's what I'm going to do. Learn to walk with my beautiful therapist."

* * *

"It's great that you can stand," said Eve one afternoon as she sat with Ben outside the hospital's main doors. She'd thought his idea about greeting people was hilarious and had made a practice of joining him whenever possible. "Maybe the reason it's so hard to take a step is psychosomatic."

Ben nodded. "Maybe, I just don't understand why. Walking's all I ever think about. I want it more than anything. I have no idea what could be blocking me from doing it. I swear it's the hardest thing I've ever tried to do."

"The hardest years in life are the ones that live upon life itself."

"What's that supposed to mean?"

Eve laughed, "I'm not sure, but it sounded good; didn't it? I think it's something Helen Hayes said. It's engraved on one of the plaques by the nurses' station."

"I know if I keep working at it, I'll figure it out. But for the life of me, I can't figure out what it is that's holding me back."

"If you rest, you rust," joked Eve.

"Don't tell me, another snippet of Ms. Hayes' wisdom."

"Yes, but it's good advice."

Ben nodded. He knew she was right. There were no quick fixes, only hard work.

With time and weeks of practice, Ben was able to put one foot in front of the other. Each day he would painfully hobble from one end of the parallel bars to the other. Though it took nearly 10 minutes to walk the five feet and back, and it hurt like hell, Ben didn't mind. This was good pain. It was the kind of pain that would eventually get him out of the hospital and back to his life.

Each night he fell asleep thinking about walking. He would often dream he was still healthy. In one dream, he was at the annual Theta Chi All Male Revue. The event always raised more than a thousand dollars for charity. For the past two years, he and Jack had MC'd the event.

In the dream, girls wildly cheered as he introduced each dancer. His brothers often tried to outdo each other with wild costumes, crazy themes, and intricate moves as they paraded across the stage, encouraging the women to bid more. At the end of the show, Jack and Ben would always strip down to their skivvies to the great delight of their audience. Then they'd all do a curtain call dance.

Ben awoke smiling to himself. He certainly had some crazy times with his brothers. A sharp pain in his legs brought him back to reality. He threw back the covers and stared at his gruesome scars. Tears stung his eyes when he saw his legs. He always hoped his imagination was worse than it really was. But no matter how many times he looked at his legs, all he could see was a monster.

He swallowed hard. There was no way he'd ever be able to MC the revue again. There was no way he could dance in front of hundreds of women looking the way he did. They'd be so repulsed, he was sure they'd start booing him or worse yet walk out. The fundraiser would be a failure all because of him!

He turned his face into the pillow. As he did so, he caught sight of the slip of paper taped to his railing.

> *The only constant in life is change. The past is behind you, the present has yet to come. The only thing you can directly control is the present moment. Enjoy striving to achieve the challenges before you now. Tough times don't last, tough people do.*

He had to stay in the moment and focus on what he really wanted… not something that might never come to pass. More than anything, he wanted to walk on his own again. He had to make it a priority. Yet even that was a frustrating thought. He was only given one hour a day for physical therapy. It simply wasn't enough to practice. How could anyone learn to walk under such restrictions?

When babies learned, they did it all the time. He just had to find a way to increase his therapy. While his insurance wouldn't allow Colleen to help him more, and it was unfair to ask her to help him for free, he wondered if there just might be another way to get in more practice time.

"I was thinking," Ben said during physical therapy the next afternoon, "I've got permission to roam the halls. What if I happened to roll down here and work out on my own? Would I be allowed to do that?"

"You mean without my supervision?" asked Colleen.

"You'd still be in the room of course. I mean, I wouldn't break in or do it in off hours or anything."

"I think it's a great idea, just as long as you understand that I can't come running over to help you every five minutes."

"I think I can manage."

"Then go for it. Even though no patient has done it before, I'd be happy to have you in here."

After that, Ben spent nearly every waking hour down in the large physical therapy room. It was the largest room on the hospital floor. The room was filled with fancy machines, with pulleys, weights, and other devices. Looking around the room one could see determined therapists pushing their visibly exhausted patients to try harder. Some of the patients were amputees, while others were working off their wheelchairs. Ben tried to look at it like a gym and he was training for some big event, like championship football game, or a weightlifting competition. The other therapists noticed his unusual determination and often came to help him when they weren't busy with other patients. Though Colleen was a favorite and therefore busier than most, Ben often caught her watching him across the room. His heart would swell during these times and he'd push himself that much harder just to make her proud.

Ben pulled himself up on to the parallel bars and started another long track down to the end and back, when he felt someone behind him. He turned to see Colleen.

"I thought you were just getting off work."

"I am, but I've noticed that you're using your upper body strength much more than you should."

"What if my legs can't take my full weight? What if I break one again?"

"Let me tell you a little secret." Colleen leaned in so close he could almost taste her perfume. "You have a titanium rod in your leg. You could hold up a car and still be fine."

He searched her eyes. "But what if..."

"Ababababa," she silenced him. "Just try it."

He gingerly took one step and then another allowing his legs to bear his full weight. Then he panicked. What if his luck ran out? What if his legs really weren't strong enough? He couldn't go through it all again.

As he tried to take another step he felt a small hand under his. He looked down to see Colleen placing her hands beneath his. Every time he tried to move or take a step, she'd quickly slide her hands under his, preventing him from using the full weight of his upper body to move himself along the bars. She knew that he would never hurt her, which forced him to make the decision to shift his weight to his legs instead of his hands.

"Hey, that's no fair. You're cheating," he accused.

"And so are you," she reminded him.

"Fair enough." Ben took a few more steps, testing out his full weight. "So if you're off the clock, why are you here?"

"Because I'm one of those really fortunate people. I get the chance to do what I love every day."

"What's that?"

"Helping patients reach their full potential."

"So that still doesn't answer why you're still here."

"I guess I had one more patient who needed to reach his full potential today."

CHAPTER TWENTY-FIVE

THE MIRACLE MAN

When Ben returned from therapy his whole family, along with Aunt Helga, Uncle Eddie, Eddie's 85-year-old mother, their children and grandchildren, his European Aunt Lottie and Uncle Jerry, cousins Judy, Yair, Adam, Michael, Arielle, Cassandra, his friend Chris, and some staff from Helen Hayes Hospital were there to greet him.

"What's going on?" he asked.

"Surprise! Happy Birthday," they all yelled.

Ben had been so wrapped up in trying to walk again, that he'd completely forgotten what day it was.

His friends and family started to sing as a hospital worker wheeled in a brightly decorated cake with twenty-two candles on it.

"You gotta make a wish," said Bruce, lowering the cake so that Ben could reach it from his wheelchair.

"That's easy," said Ben, grinning. "I wish I could..."

"Don't say it aloud," teased Cassandra, "or it won't come true."

"All right then I won't tell you that my wish has something to do with not being in this wheelchair," laughed Ben, taking in a huge breath. He leaned in and blew out all the candles at once.

"Like we can't figure this one out," joked Michelle.

"All right, who wants ice cream with their cake?" asked Doris as she pulled a scooper from the cooler she'd brought with her.

"I do!" said Bruce.

"Me too!" Debbie seconded.

"Me three!" echoed Uncle Eddie.

"Get in line behind Ben, because he's first," she smiled, handing Ben his cake and ice cream.

Ben was born 22 years earlier, on his parents' wedding anniversary. "Happy Anniversary Mom, sorry I didn't get you a present," blushed Ben.

"There is no greater gift than to have a child born on your father and my anniversary. All we need is to have you well again."

Ben looked around at the happy faces in his room. If someone had asked him last March how he would celebrate his twenty-second birthday, this wouldn't have been it. This time last year, he was celebrating by bar hopping with his fraternity brothers. He wondered if he'd ever hang out with them again like that.

* * *

The harder Ben worked, the more his coordination and ability to walk on crutches improved. As his therapy progressed, Ben wondered if he would always be on crutches, if he would walk with a limp, or if he'd ever be able to run again.

"I think you need to concentrate on your accomplishments so far," advised Dr. Hughes.

"Yes, I know all that. But what are my chances Doctor?" Ben asked solemnly.

"You've already done more than anyone I've ever seen with similar brain and orthopedic injuries. When the brain stem is damaged the way yours has been, most people never regain the neurologic function that you have. You're already a living miracle. You've beaten the odds."

But Ben didn't feel like he'd beat the odds. He wanted to do more. "Yes, but will I ever be able to walk without assistance? If so, will I ever run again?"

"I think there's no way of knowing. We will just have to wait and see."

Ben asked every doctor who examined him the same questions and they all gave similar responses.

"What do you want them to say?" asked his sister, Debbie.

"I don't know," said Ben, as he wheeled his chair up and down the hallway. "I just thought they might be a little more encouraging."

"I think they're just trying to be realistic."

"Maybe I don't want realistic. Maybe I want encouragement. It seems like every step of the way someone's been telling me 'no' or 'I can't,' or 'it's not possible.' And I've proven them wrong every single time. Why can't they give me room to dream?"

Debbie laughed. "Because you don't need their permission to accomplish the impossible. You're going to do it no matter what anyone says. You've always been like that."

"Been like what?"

"Taken on things no one else would dare to. Remember in high school when you needed a summer job so you applied to be a camp swim instructor? You knew the job was in the bag until they told you that you had to speak Japanese. The camp was for the children of Japanese businessmen! Most people would have given up and walked away, but not you."

Ben grinned. "I went out and bought some books on Japanese."

"And you studied your butt off for three weeks until camp started."

"By the time I held my first class, I knew enough Japanese water terms to be a pretty good swim teacher."

"Enough that they invited you back for four summers! I don't know too many people who could have pulled that off successfully." She leaned down eye level with her brother, "So why is this crazy dream any different?"

He shook his head. "I don't know. Maybe I'm tired of going at it all alone. Maybe I just want someone to believe in me, to tell me it's possible."

He wheeled his chair around and started back down the corridor toward his room.

Debbie frowned. "But we do believe in you. You have an entire cheering section rooting for you back home. We know if you say you're going to do something, you will."

Ben sighed, "But you're not doctors."

"What? No."

"I just wish I knew someone like me who got better."

"You do," she said, fishing in her purse. "Or at least you will when you finish reading this." She took out a book and handed it to her brother.

"*The Miracle Man* by Morris Goodman." Ben looked at his sister. "I don't get it."

"This guy Morris was a lot like you. He had it all. He was a wealthy businessman, when his plane crashed and he was paralyzed from the neck down. About the only thing he could do was blink. But he worked his way back from all that."

Ben studied the cover, which featured a picture of Goodman's plane crash. He wanted to read it as soon as possible. Maybe this guy knew something he didn't.

That night he opened the book to the first page and began to read:

What was left of the plane lay upside down. Upon impact it had flipped over, and the wings had struck the ground flat. Each wing contained a gas tank. Incredibly they had not ruptured. Sparks were everywhere; wires entangled the aircraft like a black widow's web. Several lines had set the grass on fire.

Ben read the first paragraph and then reread. Though he recognized the words, he had no idea what it said. He tried again and again. After 15 attempts, he was able to comprehend a little of it. He was reading about an accident.

He put the book down and rubbed his eyes. It saddened him to think that while he would learn to walk again, his mental disabilities would always be with him. He flipped through the pages. It wasn't that big of a book. He wondered if he'd ever be able to finish it, or if he'd just have to lie to Debbie and tell her it was a good book.

Ben thought about what he learned from being on Coach Mainieri's football team. Perhaps if he pushed himself twice as hard for as long as possible when it came to reading, it would become easier as well.

Chapter Twenty-Six

UNCLE EDDIE'S HELP

Within time, Ben was able to make it from one end of the parallel bars to the other without assistance. But at the end of his session, he was confined to his wheelchair, because other than standing, he still didn't have the skills to walk with crutches or a walker. He'd tried to use the walking aides several times, but couldn't quite get the hang of it.

The problem was that every time he tried to walk with crutches, he would fall backwards. Though he wasn't about to give up, he was ready to invest in a helmet and crash pads. He couldn't find his center of balance. How was he supposed to lean forward and yet remain standing? Everyone knew that if weight was dispersed unevenly, you would tip. It didn't make any sense to his brain or body.

But walking on crutches was his goal. It had to be. That was the key to going home. He had to be able to use the crutches independently in order to be released.

On Friday afternoon, Aunt Helga and Uncle Eddie came to visit. Uncle Eddie came to visit more than any other of Ben's relatives. Rain or shine, with or without Helga, Eddie was there. Ben had always loved Eddie. But his respect for this man, who could walk so well on an artificial leg, blew Ben away.

It also helped to have someone who really understood what he was going through. Every time he visited, Eddie always had an open ear to listen or pointers to give.

"What seems to be the problem?" asked Eddie when Ben explained his crutch dilemma.

"It's like riding a bike. I want to do it, I just can't figure out how," said Ben, biting his lip. "Do you think maybe you can show me?"

"Give it a whirl and let me see what ya got."

Aunt Helga brought Ben's crutches to him and he tried to stand. Almost immediately he fell back onto the bed.

"Hmph, is that all?" sighed Eddie with an amused look.

Ben looked at his uncle incredulously. "What do you mean 'Is that all?' I might never be able to walk again."

"Have they tried lowering the crutches?"

"What? Lowering. No, why?"

"Let me see those," said Eddie, taking one. He fiddled with the screws and made a few adjustments. Then stood them side by side. "These look even. Give 'em a try."

Ben skeptically took the crutches. He wasn't sure how adjusting them would help if his problem was balance. Slowly he stood and positioned himself over the arm cushions. They did feel better. He was so busy making sure he was standing correctly that it took him a minute to realize that he was standing all alone on crutches.

"Hey, I'm not falling!" Ben was beaming.

"Bet you can walk too," grinned Eddie, standing to brace Ben if he needed it.

But Ben didn't need it. He could walk just as easily on the crutches as he did on the parallel bars. Never once did he fall.

"This is too easy," Ben grinned. "I wonder why Colleen didn't have me do this."

Uncle Eddie shook his head, "Sometimes the simplest of solutions are the most difficult to see."

Ben was so excited, he took another lap around the room. For once it was the equipment instead of his body that was at fault! He couldn't stop smiling for the rest of the weekend. When Monday came, he was so excited to show Colleen that he was at therapy an hour before his scheduled time.

"Who did this to your crutches?" she asked when Ben showed her what he could do.

He hesitated; surprised that she wasn't blown away. "My Uncle Eddie."

"The one who lost his leg?"

"Yes, that's him."

Colleen worked with so many people with disabilities, that sometimes she forgot that she didn't really know what it was like and that she needed to listen instead of insisting they do it her way. "Well good for Uncle Eddie," she smiled.

"So then it's okay?"

"It's more than okay. It's got you up and moving. But I'm afraid you'll only be able to use your crutches during therapy. I don't want to catch you racing down the halls on these things. You're still not strong enough and I don't need you taking a tumble and going back to square one."

"Are you trying to get rid of me?" he joked.

"For months. Why are you still hanging around here?" She sobered then. "But seriously, no walking without supervision."

"What about in here after my session?"

"Not even in here. This is much more dangerous."

Ben hung his head. He thought he was making real progress. The main reason he'd come as far as he had was because he'd been allowed to practice, practice, practice. Now it was all being taken away from him.

"Tell you what," said Colleen, seeing his discouraged face. "How about I double the length of your sessions?"

"But what about my insurance?"

"Let me worry about that, I think I have a way."

From that day on, Ben was the last patient of the day. When his official hour was up, Colleen would stay an extra hour after work to help him work harder.

The extra work paid off too. Ben was allowed to leave the hospital for day trips home on the weekends. Though he was never allowed to use his crutches for these outings, it was still a big deal. He'd proudly transfer himself from his wheelchair to the car.

On his first ride home, Ben stared at the world in wide wonder. Maybe it was because he'd grown up in the same area all his life, but he'd never stopped to notice or really appreciate his surroundings. Now he gazed at the beautiful homes and perfectly manicured lawns, the graceful elegance of the trees bowing over the streets and sheltering shops, and the bright blue sky.

He'd spent an eternity confined to the hospital. Now he was falling in love with his community all over again. He again thought that he must be going through the same thing prisoners feel after spending time in jail.

The car came to a red light and stopped beside a small cemetery. Although he was familiar with the area, he'd never noticed the cemetery. He studied the slabs of marble and granite with loving epitaphs scrawled on them in old-fashioned curlicues. This is where I could be right now he thought. Cold, dead, buried six feet under and nothing but a memory. A chill ran up his spine as the car started again.

Hank had mixed emotions as he helped Ben out of the car. He was happy to have Ben back safely and yet he found it ironic that it was his son instead of him that needed the wheelchair. He'd always assumed it would be the other way around, the young man pushing the older man. A wave of sorrow washed over him.

"You all right, Dad?" Ben asked as they worked their way toward the house.

"Just happy to have you home," said Hank, patting Ben's shoulder.

A small party, including Cassandra, Aunt Helga, Uncle Eddie, cousins Judy, Yair, Adam, Michael and Arielle, greeted Ben at the house. "Surprise!" they shouted when he opened his car door. Hank had purchased a small black wheelchair for the occasion. To Ben's surprise, it was much easier to negotiate than the big wheelchair at the hospital.

Inside, there was a delicious spread of lox, bagels, and mixed salad. Everyone wanted to talk with Ben. Though he was happy to see everyone, it was difficult to repeatedly answer so many of the same questions over and over. As the guests mixed and mingled, Hank wound his way through the crowd snapping pictures and joking with everyone.

"He's really back," smiled Doris, coming up behind Hank and hugging him. "Our son is back."

He kissed her. "Yes, he is. All right, we need everyone over here for a group photo."

Doris watched as all her children gathered around. For the first time, she felt like the battle was over. Ben had conquered so much, and they'd all lived to tell. She couldn't be more proud of all of them.

Ben tried to smile as he visited with his loved ones. He had never realized how un-wheelchair friendly his house was until then. The hallways weren't wide enough, the bathroom didn't have bars for support, and worst of all, there were steps. Plenty of steps. The only way he could get up them was to sit on his butt and scoot from one to the next like a toddler.

"I could carry you," offered Bruce.

"Oh yeah, that would make things so much better," joked Ben, scooting up another step.

"I just hate to see you struggle."

"Yeah, me too. But I need to take care of myself."

By the time Ben crawled back into his bed at Helen Hayes that night, he was physically and emotionally exhausted. He was relieved to be back in the peace and solitude of his room. As he reflected on the day's events, he realized that although life at the rehabilitation hospital was much easier, nothing could compare to being back with his family in the only home he'd ever known.

CHAPTER TWENTY-SEVEN

MORE DETERMINED THAN EVER

Now that Ben had a taste of the good life at home, he worked harder than ever to get discharged. He approached therapy with a new vigor and great enthusiasm. He was more determined than ever to build his strength, master his crutches and move on to learning to climb stairs without assistance.

Climbing the stairs was the easy part. It was going down that scared the crap out of Ben. He'd never had a fear of heights, but seeing the whole flight of steps in front of him just reminded him how far he could fall with just one misstep. It always made him feel like he was falling.

Little by little, he did improve. In fact, when he looked back at his progress from the beginning of the week to the end, he could always see a dramatic difference and so could anyone he asked.

Unfortunately, the same enthusiasm didn't translate into the same level of cognitive and mental improvement. He had owned *The Miracle Man* book for more than a month and was only on page 25. Though he wanted to read the book badly, the process intimidated him. It took him forever to comprehend the most basic of concepts when he had to read. Plus, when he picked up the book to continue reading, he couldn't remember much of the story he had already read and would often have to go back to the beginning and start all over again.

"What's up champ?" asked Art one Saturday afternoon when Ben was looking particularly depressed.

Ben gave a miserable sigh. "I'm just not the same person I used to be."

Art chuckled. "None of us are. If we were, we'd all be running around in diapers."

"I mean, I used to be on the honor roll, and now I struggle to read a single paragraph. I was supposed to be a lawyer, but there's no way I'll even be able to finish my last six weeks of college. Law school is a pipe dream. I have no idea what I'm going to do with my life or how I'm going to support myself."

"Hmm, that is a tough one. But you know, your situation reminds me a little of being on a football team."

"Say what?"

"On a team everyone has their strengths and weaknesses. Some guys are great catchers, but they can't throw the ball worth a damn. Others are great runners, but can't block. Just because they can do one thing and not the other doesn't mean they're off the team, it just means they have to find the position that's right for them."

"How does that relate to me?"

"It means you're not off the team, you just need to switch positions. A football team has 22 different positions to choose from, but in life the possibilities are endless. You didn't come into this world with the pre-destination 'lawyer' stamped on your forehead. I bet there are a million things you could still do really well. You just need to take the pressure off yourself to be that one thing you decided to do years ago. Examine your possibilities."

"Like what?"

"Maybe you could sell sports equipment or coach."

"I suppose I could work in a hospital motivating patients."

Art laughed. "Not with your current attitude."

"What are you going back to school for?"

Art flashed a wide grin. "Psychology. What else!"

Throughout the long, hot summer, Ben pushed himself to excel. As soon as he realized he didn't have to finish college or become a lawyer to be successful, he was overcome with relief.

In a strange sort of way, taking the pressure off himself to have to read, made it easier to work on reading. He came at it with the mindset that he knew it was going to be messy. The point was to get through it, not to be perfect. With practice, he noticed a slight improvement. He no longer had to read each paragraph quite so many times. Fifteen became thirteen times and then ten. The harder he worked at reading, the more his comprehension skills improved. He forced himself to read in every spare minute, day or night. If he wasn't working with his crutches, he was working on his mind.

By the end of summer, Ben was discharged from Helen Hayes Hospital. He'd undergone 12 surgeries, lost more than 30 pounds, and been hospitalized for more than 130 days. He still walked with crutches, but the goal of walking without them was in sight. His reading was far from perfect, yet it had improved, and his depression was under control. Even though he had come so far, he couldn't get it out of his mind that medical science didn't support his goal of having a full and complete recovery from his brain and orthopedic injuries.

Posing with his father months before leaving for Daytona Beach, Florida.

Posing with his family (from left to right: Hank, Doris, Bruce, Michelle, Ben, Debbie) before the accident, while goofing around by standing on his toes as he would often do, to appear taller than the rest of his family.

Taken on the day of the accident having no idea of the life changing events
to occur within hours.

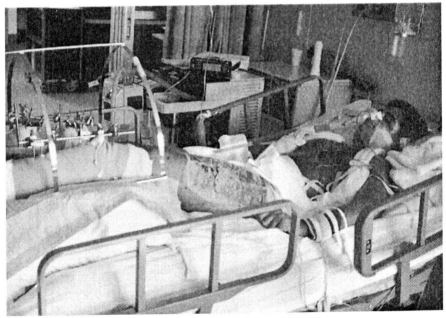

Taken days after the accident, while on full life support.
With each day, it was unknown if he would live or die.

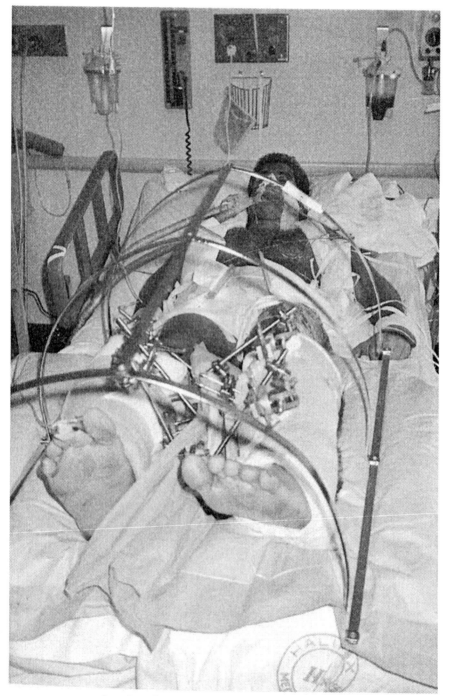

Another photograph while on full life support.

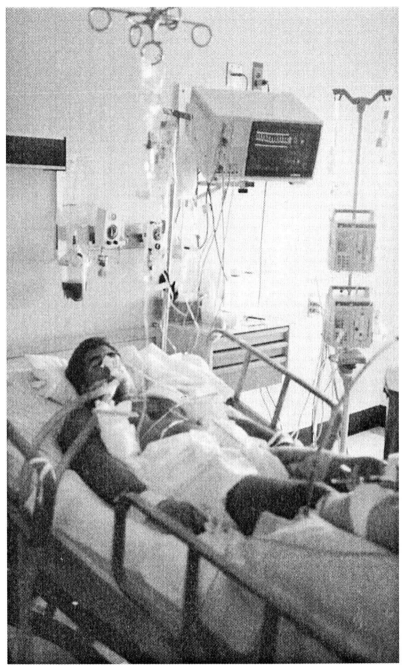

Depicting some of the many machines which were connected to monitor his comatose condition.

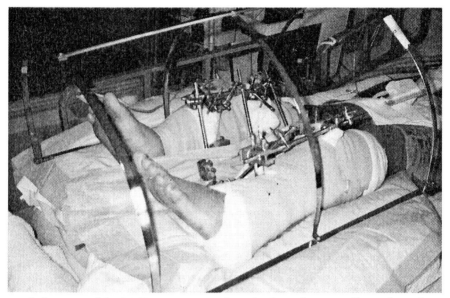

A close-up of the *Hoffman Devices* with multiple nails surgically implanted through his flesh and into his bones in an attempt to align and hopefully create a future "union" of the bones.

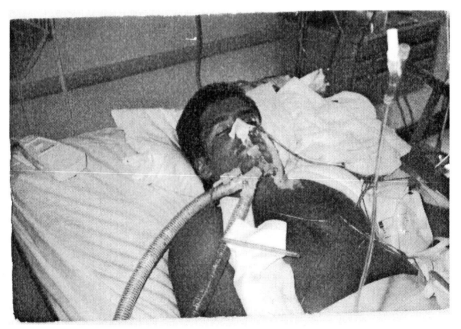

A close-up of his face, which was still tan from being on the beach days earlier.

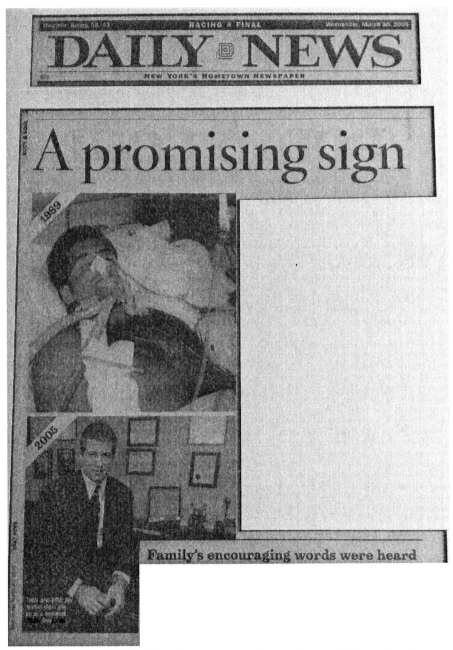

A New York Daily News feature story after study revealed benefits of communicating with the comatose.

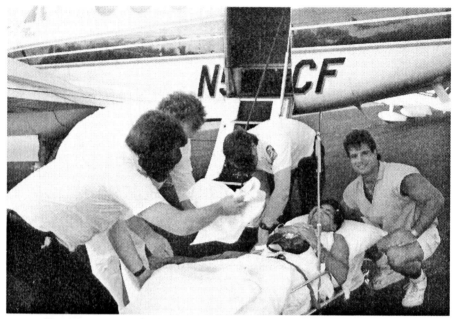

Bruce trying to relax his brother as he is being prepared to board the
unexpectedly small air ambulance.

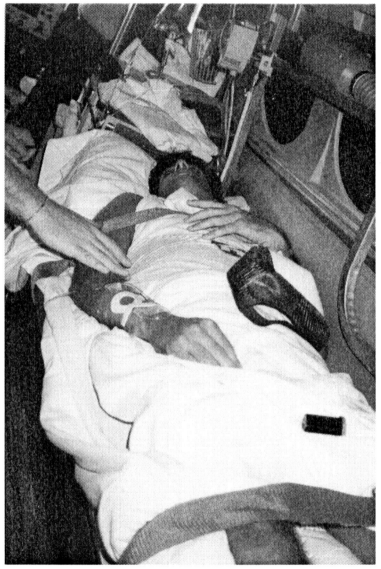

The nurse on the air ambulance trying to comfort his very
nervous and in pain patient.

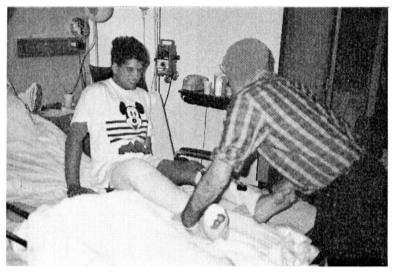

Very determined to learn the difficult skill of
transferring from his hospital bed into a wheelchair.

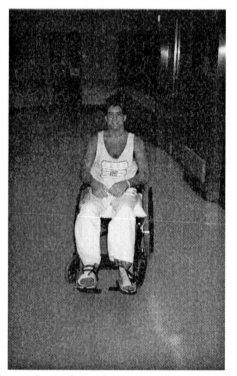

Having finally learned to independently transfer to a wheelchair provided
him with his first feeling of independence since waking from the coma.

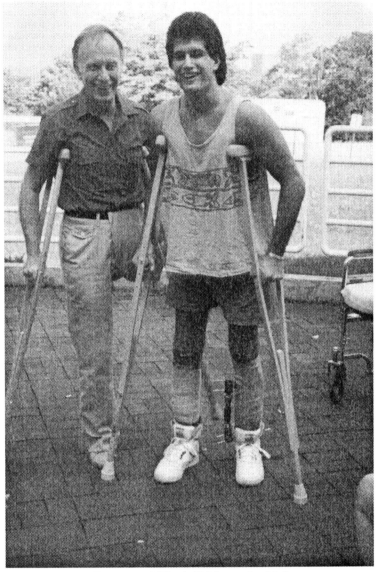

Posing with Uncle Eddie on his 22nd
birthday celebration while in the hospital.

Happily being discharged from Helen Hayes Hospital not realizing that he would be returning later in the year.

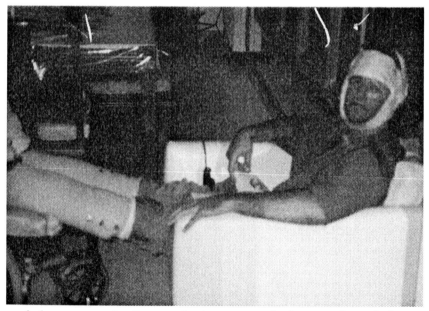

At home recovering from an elective surgery which was performed after having returned to college. He didn't realize at the time that this surgery would be the reason for his return to in-patient hospitalization.

Having dinner with Dawn and his two (2) kids in the same
pizza restaurant at which he proposed to Dawn years earlier.

Happily posing with his family during one of his annual
vacations to Ocean City, Maryland.

To the surprise of the orthopedic surgeons, participating in the daily run with the goal of exceeding pre-accident speeds. (Photo by taken by Laura)

PART THREE

NEW LIFE

Go for it now. The future is promised to no one.

~ Dr. Wayne Dyer, psychologist and motivational speaker

CHAPTER TWENTY-EIGHT

HOME AT LAST

Montvale, New Jersey, July

Even though Ben had weekend visits home, it felt like he had been gone for years when he returned for good. Everything somehow seemed different, like it didn't quite fit anymore. He felt naked without the security of the hospital's special equipment. Hank and Doris had done their best to outfit the house with special seats for the shower and toilet, as well as cleared large paths through highly traveled areas to accommodate his crutches.

Life at home was also a lot faster-paced than it had been at the hospital and Ben had a long to-do list. He planned on going back to school in the fall to finish his last six weeks and so arrangements had to be made with all his professors.

Eager to get rid of his ugly facial and leg scars, he also made arrangements to meet with Bruce's plastic surgeon. Not that Bruce had had a lot of reconstructive surgery, but a few years back he'd gotten into a bar fight and needed stitching up. When he got to the ER, he'd insisted on waiting for a plastic surgeon as opposed to a random trauma doctor. He waited 12 hours for the plastic surgeon to arrive in the emergency room, but it was well worth the wait. He'd raved about the doctor ever since and even joked that he'd made him even better looking than before the fight.

With as many specialists and research as Ben had had to do over the months to find needed help, he felt fortunate to have firsthand knowledge of such a good doctor. Surgery was scheduled for later that fall, after he had a good grip on his schoolwork. Nothing could make Ben feel more independent than being able to drive again. Even though he believed he had regained the necessary skills to drive, he first wanted to make the attempt with an experienced driver by his side, just in case his confidence wasn't realistic.

Then there were the visiting nurses that stopped by several times a week. Ben still had a heparin lock in his arm, used to hook up the IVs for his ongoing leg infection, and he'd developed a painful rash under his arms from using the crutches so much.

He also attended daily physical therapy sessions at Pascack Valley Hospital, a few miles from his home. The goal, as always, was to help him walk independently. Every morning a service van would pick him up and take him into the hospital. Ben looked at therapy as if he was going to work.

"I've been thinking," Ben said to Hank in his study after dinner one evening. "It would be much easier for me if I could drive myself to and from the hospital. Do you think the doctors would let me?"

"I've never thought about it."

"I know I could do it. My feet work fine. I mean, I can feel them and I can move my legs, therapy's really only to improve strength, range of motion and balance."

"I suppose we could ask."

"Thanks Dad."

Ben watched as Hank picked up his magazine, but made no move to leave.

"Yes?" Hank lowered the publication.

"I probably won't be able to drive again right away, will I? I'll need to practice first."

"Probably."

"Sooo will you take me, if they say yes?"

Hank smiled. He was so proud of his son that had come so far in just a few short months. "You know I will."

A wide grin spread across Ben's face. He was coming back to himself more and more. "Thanks Dad."

The doctors gave Ben the go-ahead and he and Hank began practicing driving again. Because it didn't involve great physical strength, and his Trans Am was automatic, he was driving in no time. Each morning he would haul himself into physical therapy and when the day was done, he'd drive himself home.

Being stationary for so many months meant that Ben's legs and ankles had lost their flexibility. So he'd spend the better part of the morning increasing his range of motion through a series of painful bending and twisting exercises.

When the flexing was finished, he worked on walking with a cane. But the new device presented two problems. First, Ben's balance was still quite compromised. The crutches had created an extra set of limbs, which helped him to balance like a tripod, but the cane was less stable. Second, his brain couldn't compute the new set of motions required to walk with the cane. He continuously tried to move his right arm and leg together instead of using his opposite limbs together.

After several weeks of therapy, Ben mastered the art of walking with a cane. The only problem was his balance was so delicate that if someone slightly brushed against him, he easily toppled over.

"Dude, we should celebrate," grinned Jack when Ben showed off his new ability. "A toast," he said, raising his can of Coke.

"Yeah, I don't know if that's such a great idea."

"Why not?" Jack asked, taking a sip.

"Because I don't want people to stare. It will draw attention."

"Because it's totally cool."

"Yeah right. I look like an old man," said Ben taking a long gulp.

"No way, all those British dudes use them, when they visit the Queen and stuff. It's very debonair."

Ben choked and nearly blew Coke out his nose. "Debonair? Since when do you use words like that?"

"Since I've been hanging out with the Queen," said Jack, making a deep bow and stumbling over his own feet.

"Sure you have."

* * *

Now that Ben could drive, he felt freer than he ever had in his lifetime. On days when he didn't have therapy, he would drive around with his car's T-tops off and appreciate the beauty of the world outside of the hospital.

One Saturday, he was driving in his hometown, Montvale, and drove by the town park. He instantly remembered playing at that field with his friends from town every summer Saturday since junior high school. He was immediately overwhelmed with fear and sadness about his no longer being able to join the guys who were playing basketball there that Saturday. He wondered whether he should turn around to see the guys. Being that the guys hadn't seen him since playing with him last summer, he was afraid to show his face and immediately cause them to change their memory of his being one of their fast and athletic teammates.

After gathering his composure, Ben turned the car around and drove to the Montvale Town Park. The same guys Ben had played games of pick-up basketball and softball with since junior high were all there. Some came over to see how he was doing, while others just yelled things like, "long time no see," and "great to have you back."

Ben watched as his friends ran up and down the court, shouting and laughing. Life was so easy for them, the way they ran, dribbled the ball, and even dodged each other. They had no idea how lucky they all were.

He sniffed the air, full of sweat, tanning oil, and the dry leaves of the coming fall. The year certainly had not turned out as he had planned. He slowly stood and walked back to his car. He was glad his friends were so happy, but he couldn't stay and watch. It just reminded him of what he couldn't do anymore.

* * *

Ben awkwardly picked up the phone, dialed the number, and waited for someone to pick up.

"Mothers Against Drunk Driving, may I help you?"

"Hi. My name is Ben and I was in a bad accident in Florida caused by a drunk driver. The Florida Chapter of M.A.D.D. really helped my family, so I'm calling to see if I can get more involved with M.A.D.D. here in New Jersey. The only problem is, I'm not a mother and don't think that will ever change."

The voice on the other end began with a chuckle, "I'm Florence Nass, president of the local New Jersey Chapter of Mothers Against Drunk Driving. Don't worry; there is nothing in our bylaws that requires active members to be a mother, or a father for that matter. Most new members become involved because they were touched by drunk driving one way or another. All you have to be is an adult committed to ending drinking and driving. My husband and I first started this chapter in New Jersey because of our very tragic loss of our son Michael. He was killed by a drunk driver."

"I'm so sorry," said Ben. "If there's anything I can do…"

"Actually, there is. You're quite the celebrity here at our chapter. We've followed your story closely."

Ben blushed. He was aware that several stories had run about him in area papers and on TV. Though a few reporters had even interviewed him, he hadn't realized how many other people saw them too.

"M.A.D.D. was so supportive during my recovery; I'd really like to give back."

"It would be great to meet you. Why don't you come to our upcoming televised ceremony? I would love it if you came up on stage so we could welcome you to our M.A.D.D. New Jersey family."

Ben was uncomfortable about being televised in front of a bunch of people while using his crutches.

"We've already got NFL kicker Ali Haji-Sheikh as our celebrity speaker."

Ben smiled at the thought of sharing the stage with a famous football player and doing his part to help stop drunk driving at the same time. It was a deal too good to pass up. "All right, you've got a deal."

When the day for the M.A.D.D. ceremony arrived, Ben showed'up excited to be at the event. As soon as he arrived, he walked directly up to Florence Nass to meet her for the first time. He approached her, smiled, and gave her a big hug. "Hi, my name is…"

"Ben, it's so nice to finally meet you. Thank you for coming. I was wondering; being that our NFL star hasn't arrived yet, would you mind sharing your story with the crowd?"

"Me? Today? I didn't have any time to prepare. What would I say?"

"Just be yourself and you will do fine," assured Florence.

A few minutes later, Ben was invited onto the podium to address the crowd. As Ben nervously approached the microphone on his crutches, he wondered what it was that he was going to say. He walked directly to the podium, took a deep breath, and then announced his intentions to speak to M.A.D.D. groups and to do what he could to end drinking and driving.

Later that summer, he fulfilled his promise to Florence Nass and his local chapter of M.A.D.D. Speaking on behalf of drunk driving victims and survivors gave him a greater sense of fulfillment than anything he'd ever done before. Finally, he felt as if he was doing something to put an end to preventable accidents like his.

Now that he had spoken, he had to keep doing it whenever and wherever he could. He dreamed that his words would somehow impact members of the audience in ways that might someday save their lives or the lives of those around them.

CHAPTER TWENTY-NINE

BACK TO SCHOOL

"I was so pleased to hear you would be returning to us. I can hardly wait to read your paper. It's not often an undergraduate tackles such an advanced subject," smiled Professor Marshall.

Ben nodded, afraid to speak too much and give away his new mental shortcomings.

Before the accident, he'd petitioned the economics professor to do a written project on the economic foundations of marketing. Professor Marshall had tried to discourage him from the lofty subject. "Are you sure you can handle this?" he'd asked. "There aren't a great deal of reference materials readily available. It will involve a great deal of research and footwork."

But Ben had always prided himself on accomplishing the impossible. Who could have seen the obstacle that would be laid down in his path in the eleventh hour? He was grateful that the majority of the project was already finished. Still, he wasn't even sure he could handle this last little bit. It had taken him nearly five months just to finish reading *The Miracle Man*.

He'd had every intention of asking the professor to switch to something lighter and more manageable, but how could he disappoint the man who'd granted him the opportunity to do such advanced work?

The visits to each of Ben's other five professors went similarly. He could pick up most of his work where he'd left off before spring break, but he wouldn't need to attend classroom activities. Instead, he would finish his projects alone and meet with his professors twice a week to ask questions, receive needed help, and deliver progress reports.

In every case, the courses had to be tailored to his special needs. For example, in psychology, he'd been working on a project based on his experiences as a resident hall director. But he was no longer a resident director, so he no longer had daily interactions to draw from. Instead, the professor was kind enough to allow him to instead do an outline of his future goal to end drinking and driving.

He smiled wistfully thinking about how smart Coach Mainieri's rule had once made him. He'd carried a 3.56 grade point average throughout his college career. The goal for his last semester had been to finally land a perfect 4.0, which would boost his overall G.P.A. to 3.65, the minimum needed to graduate with high honors. Now that dream, let alone passing his classes, was virtually impossible.

"What am I going to do?" Ben asked Jack shortly before school started.

"Give it a shot and see what happens. Like they always say, you'll never know…"

"My point is…" Ben cut him off and then stopped short. "I ah… ah…oh crap! What was I talking about?"

"I don't know man, I forgot too," laughed Jack.

Ben shook his head. He knew his friend was well intentioned, but it drove him crazy when people said they forgot too just because he'd forgotten. It was so frustrating to lose what you were thinking and then spend the next several minutes, or even hours, trying to recall it?

Because his memory was so poor, he'd developed the habit of having to speak immediately, often interrupting others in an attempt to get the thought out before it evaded him. He knew it was annoying, but he honestly couldn't think of a way around it. Any slight interruption, a phone ringing, someone new coming into the room, a loud ad on TV, would result in whatever he'd been thinking or talking about to leave him.

As the date for school grew closer, Ben's fears about returning grew. He was ashamed of the person he'd become. How would his friends and teachers view him? How long before they realized he was not the same person who'd left them early the last school year?

There were bright spots, however. He no longer needed to take antibiotics, which meant he was no longer tethered to an IV pole. He'd also mastered walking with a cane. While he still thought it made him look like an old man, Jack assured him it was the height of cool.

"Dude, just remember if anyone asks, it's not a cane. It's a walking stick."

Ben chuckled. "They all know it's a cane."

"I wouldn't be surprised if you started a new trend. Just wait, by the end of semester everyone will be using one."

"Awesome, now I'm responsible for lowering the bar for the entire school."

"I'm picking up mine tomorrow," joked Jack.

"Great, see if you can return mine when you go."

While Jack didn't make good on his walking stick promise, he was there to help Ben on his first day back on campus. It was a warm September day with sunny, blue skies and the faint smell of drying leaves in the air. Students in acid-washed jeans, neon t-shirts, and miniskirts flooded the campus, making it seem so much more alive than when Ben had visited only a week before.

"Welcome back man," greeted a fraternity brother in the parking lot.

"Hey Ben, great to see you," smiled a pretty blonde as she passed him.

"Wow! I remember her! I didn't even think she knew my name," Ben said to Jack.

"Are you kidding? After that benefit they held for you last spring, you're a celebrity."

Ben blushed. "No one remembers that."

"Ben!" cried a brunette. "You're alive!"

"Great to see you," Ben braced himself as a petite girl wrapped her arms around him. Ben concentrated as hard as he could to remember her name, but it just didn't come to him.

"I was so worried about you," she said giving him a good squeeze.

"We all were," said Roger, Molly's boyfriend. He clapped Ben on the back. "Welcome back, buddy."

Jack quickly moved closer to Ben to keep him from falling over. He was still quite unsteady on his feet and the smallest thing could knock him off balance. To compensate, Ben got into the habit of bracing himself whenever anyone looked like they were going to hug him or pat him on the back.

"Thanks," Ben said. "I'll catch up with you later. I've got to get to Marshall's office."

"See, what'd I tell you. You are a celebrity!" assured Jack.

"Ben? Is that really you?" interrupted tall guy with curly hair.

"Hi," grinned Ben.

Frank caught Ben in a half hug. "It's so good to see you. I was so sorry to hear about the accident."

"Thanks, it's good to be back." As Ben said it, he realized it was true. All his worrying had been for nothing. At least three-dozen students, faculty, and staff greeted him on that first walk through campus. Everyone had a handshake, hug, or kind word.

It almost felt like old times again. So much so, that Ben found himself looking for other students in his year. But the students from his original graduating class were nowhere to be found. "They're gone," Ben said to himself. While he logically knew that they had graduated and moved on to their new careers or graduate school, he had somehow expected them to be there. While time raced on for them, it stood still for him. His gut twinged as reality hit him. He'd been left behind, a shell of his former self.

As if to emphasize the point, he was now in a special dorm room designed for physically disabled students. His new accommodations were located on the first floor, so that he wouldn't have to negotiate stairs. Ben shoved the door open and looked around the place trying to decide what to do first.

"Nice digs," said a familiar voice behind him.

Ben turned to see his old boss, Anne. She'd slimmed down considerably. "Wow, you look great."

"Jenny Craig can do wonders for a girl," she laughed turning in a circle. "I've lost 50 pounds so far."

"Good for you. I've lost 30 pounds on a crash diet."

She laughed as she grabbed him in a hug. "I've missed your corny humor." Then she kissed his cheek and added, "You scared the hell out of me."

"It was pretty scary for me too."

"I had to fire Ralph, you know. He and Ted actually risked their secure campus jobs and drove all the way down to see you as soon as they heard about your accident."

"I heard about that. I was so touched to hear that Ralph and Ted put their jobs on the line and drove a thousand miles just to come see me. Even though we were technically coworkers, although I never told them, I always considered Ralph and Ted to be close friends of mine. As comforting as it is to know that they probably felt the same way about me, I feel really bad that they got in trouble for making the trip. Did Ted get fired too?"

"I would've had to let him go as well, except he wasn't technically on duty and I was already down two people," she smiled. "But you're back now. That's what matters." She took his hand and led him further into the room. "What do you think of your new place?"

It was extra wide for wheel chairs and had special bars in the bathroom for showering and more in the room. Though it was a nice enough room, it was a far cry from the one-bedroom apartment, with its own living room and kitchen, which he had lived in as a residence hall director.

He gave a little nod as a lump rose in his throat. He knew things were different, but the room was even more of a reminder.

"Oh honey," Anne said, hugging Ben's shoulders. "It's going to be all right. You'll get through this and I'll be right here if you need me. We all will."

While Ben's friends were very supportive, his new college experience was very different from the carefree days of the past four years. He no longer had time to socialize or flirt with pretty co-eds. It was probably better that he didn't anyway. He was constantly mixing up memories. He could never recall which story came from which brother when he visited his fraternity. It was so important to him to give the impression of the same smart, well-rounded person he'd been before the accident, that he didn't talk nearly as much as he used to. It wasn't that he didn't want to, but every time he opened his mouth he forgot words. That always made people supply words to help the conversation flow more smoothly, which made Ben, who'd previously had an extensive vocabulary, feel like a major putz. To cover, the topics he discussed became very selective. He just couldn't get the doctors' cautions about limited improvement for those who sustain severe brain damage out of his head.

That night, Ben went to the first monthly Theta Chi Fraternity meeting. As soon as he walked into the classroom where his brothers met, he was smothered with hugs and affection from the guys who had been his core friends since before the accident.

"We all felt so helpless when you had your accident, now just look at you. Your story's nothing short of remarkable. And we all can say we knew you when. You're a real life hero and we're proud to know you," Jake said.

"We all voted and want you to be our nominee for this year's homecoming king. When we voted for our nomination, you were the choice, hands down."

Ben looked from one friend to another in disbelief.

"You're kind of like our hero, man," said Patrick.

"But I don't want to be a hero just because I was injured."

Jake shook his head, "Don't you get it? It's not because you got hurt, it's because of everything you've done since then. That's what a Theta Chi is…that's what everyone at this school wants to be. That's why we want you to represent our fraternity at this year's homecoming game."

"It would be wrong if you didn't run," added Patrick.

Ben bit his lip. He was too self-conscious to be the center of attention, and yet he knew he'd be letting a lot of people down if he didn't run. He inhaled deeply. "Okay, I'll do it on one condition. Even though every other organization does it for their nominee, I don't want anyone to campaign for me. I don't want any posters or signs up around campus. I don't want to see any fliers, and I'm not going to participate in any candidate activities. But you can leave my name on the ballot. I totally understand if you want to nominate and campaign for another brother, but that's the only offer I'll make on the subject."

The guys looked at each other.

"What do you think?" asked Patrick.

Jake tried to read Ben's face. "I don't know."

"Well I do," said Jack looking at his best friend. "I think we better take it."

* * *

Ben tackled his last six weeks of college like he had tackled football in the early days. He spent every night in the library, putting hours into completing what he previously could have done in under an hour. He also found an outpatient therapy center nearby, because he didn't want his physical improvements to be slowed because of his studies.

As the weeks progressed, he realized he could make it through. The work was more difficult than anything he'd ever undertaken, but he was developing coping techniques. He reminded himself each time he had to reread something that he was one step closer to passing his classes. "Slow and steady wins the race," he would often remind himself, quoting Aesop's famous fable about the *Tortoise and the Hare*. Graduation was possible. It just might take him a whole semester to accomplish his goal of finishing the last six weeks of college work.

One goal he wouldn't have long to wait for was plastic surgery. He planned to have a quick procedure to reduce the raised scar over his eye. At the same time, Dr. Maslowski would insert four (4) narrow balloons, known as "tissue expanders," in his leg and under his healthy skin, which would be inflated over time to expand that good skin. Then when there was enough new good skin, the old, translucent grafted skin would be removed from his leg and the new skin would be folded into place.

As the surgery date approached, Ben's excitement about losing his accident scars turned to fear about returning to the hospital. He had been out for several months and gotten a taste of the good life. No matter how beneficial the upcoming surgery would be, it involved returning to the hospital, which reminded him of the nightmare he had left behind.

Excitement filled the campus in the days before homecoming. The class schedule was lighter than usual to give students a chance to participate in preparation activities, which lent to the party atmosphere. No matter where Ben went, boom boxes blasted as excited students and alumni busily decorated with balloons, streamers, and huge homecoming court posters.

The day of the game was perfect. The air was crisp, but it was still warm enough to be comfortable. Ben invited his parents and Cassandra to enjoy the event with him.

"Do you know this is the first time we've ever been to campus for a nonacademic award?" laughed Doris, spreading a blanket on the bleachers.

"What do you know, another first," said Hank taking a seat.

Football players in blue and gold uniforms burst through a paper ring as they announced the starting lineup.

"Come on Ben, where's your school spirit?" Doris asked Ben while sitting in the stands before the game.

"For the first time since being nominated last month, I'm starting to get nervous about it. "

"Why would you be nervous?" asked Hank.

"For one thing, I'm the only candidate that didn't have posters or school ads asking for my vote. I'm going to feel like I let the fraternity down if I don't even wind up one of the three runner-ups. Also, it's been uncomfortable enough to walk through campus using a cane or crutches; I don't know how I'm going to feel walking on the football field with all the other homecoming candidates in front of 10,000 cheering fans."

Ben shook his head and settled in to watch the game. He felt almost as if he were in a movie as he sat watching the tiny figures move gracefully across the field. The smell of popcorn and hotdogs filled the air, as people juggled for better positions to see the game. Somehow everything seemed to go into hyper focus for Ben. The colors were richer, smells more intense, every detail amplified.

Cassandra nudged Ben. "I think it's getting close to half-time."

Ben stood, "Mom, Dad, we better get going."

"Now how are we going to know when it starts?" asked Doris.

"They'll call our names when it's time," Ben answered, smoothing his suit.

"Yes, but what's the order?"

"We don't know, Mom. We find out as they announce us."

And then the moment came, "Ladies and Gentleman, we now would like to introduce this year's homecoming king and queen candidates. Would the candidates and their escorts please walk onto the football field and form a semicircle facing the home team bleachers."

Ben, with Cassandra at his side, carefully walked using crutches onto the football field with the 30 other candidates representing their specific organizations. He could hear his fraternity brothers cheering for him in the background. When a perfect semicircle of candidates and their escorts were formed, all turned to face the crowd.

Ben's heart began to race as the loudspeaker announced the 3rd runner up, then the 2nd, then the 1st runner up. One by one, they would step forward to the center, receive a plaque, and then turn around to return with their escort and walk back to the semicircle.

Ben was disappointed that he was not at least selected as a runner-up and felt regret for not allowing his fraternity brothers to advertise for him over the past month. He wished there was a way for him to discreetly walk off the field without his fraternity brothers seeing him.

The crowd then became very quiet when it was announced, "Ladies and gentleman, we are at the point that you all have been waiting for. Please join me in congratulating this year's homecoming queen and king. First, this year's homecoming queen, representing the college's cheerleading team, is Nicole Bonners!" Ben observed the crowd cheer and throw confetti as Nicole gracefully waved as she walked to the center podium to be given her homecoming queen crown.

"And ladies and gentlemen, please join me in congratulating this year's homecoming king, representing Theta Chi fraternity, Ben Nevets!" Ben's heart skipped a beat. Had he won homecoming king without campaigning? The world went into slow motion as Ben walked with Cassandra to the center podium to receive his crown. Ben was the homecoming king!

The experience was overwhelming for Ben. As the former homecoming king was taking his crown off and placing it on Ben's head, with thousands in the crowd including his parents continuing to cheer, Ben felt his eyes watering up with tears of happiness. He really had come so far in only 10 months. Nothing was going to stop him now.

Chapter Thirty

PLASTIC SURGERY

Just before Thanksgiving, Ben underwent the optional plastic surgery. It was a simple procedure, which promised to have him back up and on his feet after a long weekend. But the surgery took longer than expected, lasting more than five hours.

Ben awoke in the recovery room in so much pain, that it felt as if he hadn't been given anesthesia or painkillers. It felt as if someone had bitten off a piece of his face. He could feel every inch of the long incision in his leg, which felt like it had been set on fire.

He tried to get the attention of a passing nurse, but his throat was so dry from the tube that had been inserted during the procedure that all that came out was a dusty wheeze.

Ben struggled to reach the call button, but got light-headed when he tried to sit up. White-hot pain shot through his head, burning a fiery trail across his face. He slumped back in exhaustion, hoping he would pass out.

"Hey, you're finally awake," said Hank as he appeared by Ben's bedside.

Ben moaned and tried to tell his father that he was in the worst pain of his life. But all that came out was the faintest of whispers.

Hank leaned low to hear, and then wrinkled his brow. "They've already given you a large dose of morphine. You shouldn't be in any pain."

Ben shook his head ever so slightly and mouthed the word, "No." Tears slid silently down Ben's face as the excruciating pain tore through his body, growing more intense by the second. He wished he'd thought to bring Michelle's moon with him.

Hank flagged down a doctor. "Isn't there anything you can do?" he pleaded.

Dr. Maslowski looked at Ben's chart, "He's already received the maximum dose." He tested Ben's reflexes and listened to his heart race. "In rare cases, morphine doesn't work on some people. It appears Ben is one of those people."

"Then give him something else," Hank said. "What about Demerol? We know that works."

The doctor looked at Ben and Hank grimly. "Unfortunately, we can't give Ben anything else until the morphine is out of his system. If we do, the mixture of drugs could be fatal."

"How long do we have to wait?" asked Hank, barely containing himself.

Dr. Maslowski checked his watch. "About four hours."

As the minutes ticked by, Ben thought he would go mad with pain. He thrashed and writhed unable to control his body; certain he would have a seizure at any moment. The extreme agony took him to the edge of delirium, never quite pushing him over, holding him a lucid prisoner of misery and torture.

Ben began to wish that he would die, so that the pain would end. He cursed himself for being so vain as to want his old face back. It served him right for not accepting what he had become. The only thing that kept him going was knowing every minute that went by was one step closer to getting the Demerol. If he could make it through this, he could make it through anything.

By the time a nurse came to administer the shot, Ben had visualized the moment so often, he was no longer sure if she was real or just a figment of his imagination. Then just like that, his pain subsided into a distant memory. Within an hour he was cleared to go home.

But Ben's relief was short-lived. On the ride home, his pain returned. This time he also had a very strong urge to urinate. The hospital had given him a portable urinal, which he attempted to use in the back seat as they drove down the highway. No matter how much he concentrated, he couldn't do it. At first he thought it was because of the strangeness of the whole thing. It just seemed unnatural to pee zooming down the highway at 65 miles an hour. But when you gotta go, you gotta go. Besides, he'd peed plenty of times on the side of the road as a kid. This was definitely different. He wasn't having performance anxiety. He really couldn't go. The worst of it was that he could feel his bladder expanding. He was certain it might explode at any minute.

When Ben arrived home, Bruce carried him to his room. He lay in bed in horrible pain, unable to urinate. He was so desperate to go that he convinced himself that if he wet the bed, it would be worth it. But even that didn't help. No matter how hard he tried, nothing came out. It wasn't until 36 hours after surgery that he was finally able to go. He later learned that anesthesia inhibits one's ability to go.

The elective surgery was only supposed to keep Ben out of college for an extra day. But just two days later, he woke up with his lower leg swollen to the size of his thigh. Pungent ooze seeped from a deep depression in his lower leg. As soon as he saw it, he knew the M.R.S.A. had returned. Within hours, he was in the plastic surgeon's office.

Dr. Maslowski shook his head when he saw the infection. "There's always a risk with surgery. You might want to look away." He pulled a wickedly sharp set of scissors from a tray.

Ben looked away just as he heard a snap. Before he could stop himself, he turned to see what was happening. A large amount of clear, reddish liquid gushed out of his leg, covering the office floor.

"If I was a betting man, I'd say it's M.R.S.A. We better admit you to the medical center immediately."

Ben caught his breath. He'd known in his heart, but had hoped against hope that Dr. Maslowski would offer a more positive explanation.

Once settled in his room, it felt as if no time had passed since the accident. Ben met with an infectious disease doctor who confirmed the infection had returned and that he would have to stay in the hospital and undergo aggressive IV antibiotic therapy for four to six weeks until he was out of danger, or risk losing his leg.

His life was being stolen from him again. There was no way he would be able to complete college and graduate by the end of the semester.

One week into his stay, a nurse he had never seen before entered his room. "Good morning. Dr. Aldridge asked me to set up a meeting with you this afternoon."

"But my doctor is Dr. Maslowski." Ben frowned.

The nurse looked at his chart. "No, he wants to see you. Dr. Aldridge is an orthopedist."

Ben's frown increased. He was in the hospital for an infection, not a bone problem.

"He'll be coming by this afternoon right after lunch," she smiled.

Ben nodded and turned to dial his father. If an orthopedist wanted to see him, It couldn't be good. Ben was too physically and emotionally weak to ask any more questions about his condition. Better to have his father with him to ask the tough questions.

Hank arrived just a few minutes before Dr. Aldridge walked in. He was tall and very young looking, though Ben guessed he had to be in his thirties. Long and lanky, he looked like he should have been running a marathon instead of being in a hospital.

Though he looked like a boy athlete, he was all business. "I wanted to meet with you because your M.R.I. images and blood tests indicate that your M.R.S.A. has spread to your bone."

"What exactly does that mean?" asked Hank.

"It means that Ben has developed osteomyelitis."

Hank and Ben looked at him blankly.

"It's an infection that kills bone. It will continue to eat away at the Ben's tibia until the infected area is removed. The only way to stop it is to remove the infected bone."

Ben heart drummed in his chest. "You want to amputate my leg?"

Dr. Aldridge grinned, "No, nothing quite that dramatic. There's a fascinating new device called the Taylor Spatial, which was developed in Russia. It's very promising for this type of disease. We would cut the infected bone out then attach the spatial with a series of thin nails to help fuse the healthy bone back together. Each day you would turn the nails a prescribed amount. Over the course of several months your bone would stretch back to its proper length."

Ben bit his lip. "It sounds painful."

"I'm not going to lie to you. It will be very painful, but it is the best chance you have to save your leg."

"And how many times have you actually done this new procedure?" Hank asked.

"Two or three times," smiled Dr. Aldridge.

Hank snorted. "By two or three you most likely mean once."

"Are you accusing me of lying?" asked Dr. Aldridge.

"No. Simply stating the facts. Most people have a tendency to over-state their qualifications. I want to make sure my son has the best care possible. Is there someone on staff who could give us a second opinion?"

"Don't you trust me?"

"The issue isn't about trust, it's about competence."

"This is ridiculous," said Aldridge. "I'm offering you a chance at the best and newest procedure in the world."

"If it's the best, then I want someone else to confirm it before you go sawing my son's leg in half."

Aldridge's eyes blazed. "I am the leading orthopedist at this hospi-tal!"

Ben's cheeks grew red at the exchange and he tried to shrink into the background as his father argued with the doctor.

"Then one of your colleagues shouldn't have a difficult time confirm-ing your diagnosis."

"I won't be second guessed by someone who knows less than I do."

"Then you won't be touching Ben's leg."

"And you have made a grave mistake." Dr. Aldridge looked at Ben before storming out. "Remember this when you're left with no option but to amputate."

Ben watched the doctor go in shock. "Dad?" he asked with growing concern.

"Gather your things Ben. We're going to take you back to Helen Hayes," said Hank calmly.

Chapter Thirty-One

HELEN HAYES REVISITED

"I can't tell you how disappointed I am that you went ahead with this surgery without consulting me," said Dr. Hughes.

"I'm sorry," said Ben hanging his head. The doctor was right of course, but it had never even occurred to Ben to consult an orthopedist on plastic surgery issues. The two didn't even seem connected.

"About the osteomyelitis," Hank began, but Dr. Hughes cut him off.

"Who says Ben has osteomyelitis?"

"Dr. Aldridge did," Hank answered with a frown.

"I wouldn't be so sure about that. One should never make such a serious diagnosis based on an M.R.I. and a few blood tests. Too many diseases and infections have similar symptoms."

"So what do I have?" asked Ben.

"Let's find out. I want you to stand on your infected leg."

Ben thought it was a peculiar request, but obliged. "Hey, it doesn't hurt!"

"Now throw down your crutches and walk my son," Dr. Hughes joked in a dramatic voice.

Ben slowly put his crutches down as Dr. Hughes held his arm and helped him walk around the office.

"Now hold my arms and hop on your 'infected' leg." Ben again felt strange as he hopped while holding another man's arms.

"Just as I thought," the doctor smiled. "If you had osteomyelitis, your leg wouldn't be able to support you and would give out after a short while."

"So what is wrong with me then?"

"I think the M.R.S.A. has returned in the form of a deep tissue infection. You've had M.R.S.A. for so long, that the images on an M.R.I. could be deceiving to an untrained eye. But we'll go ahead and schedule a biopsy of your bone just to make sure nothing else is going on. Being that you will be back on Vancomycin for several weeks, while you're under anesthesia, I recommend that another surgeon insert a central venous catheter. This will allow you to receive I.V. treatment at home, instead of in the hospital. And there will be no need to stick you every three days to replace the heparin lock in your arm to funnel the IV antibiotics."

"What about that Dr. Aldridge?" asked Hank. "Shouldn't we do something about him?"

"It's a violation of the Hippocratic Oath to operate on a patient whose condition doesn't warrant surgery, but there's no evidence that he knew he shouldn't. Many young doctors are overzealous and eager to try out new procedures. The important thing now is that you had the forethought to ask for a second opinion and Ben is getting the help he needs now."

Ben prayed the night before the surgery that the biopsy would be negative. After all that he had been through, he could not imagine how he would muster up the energy to deal with the major surgery that would be required if the biopsy came back positive for M.R.S.A. in his tibia bone.

Ben was delighted to learn that the biopsy came back as negative. He was soon discharged from the hospital with a central venous catheter attached to his chest. In the weeks that followed, Ben stayed at home with visiting nurses coming three times per week to replenish the Vancomycin and flush his central venous catheter.

The entire plastic surgery and infection scare lasted six weeks, which delayed college graduation for yet another semester.

"Forget about it," Bruce said trying to comfort Ben.

He nodded. "I already have. To tell the truth, I'm not exactly in any big hurry to start law school. I still have no idea how I'm going to get through a doctorate program with my brain damage and permanent cognitive disabilities. An extra semester of undergrad is just fine with me."

"If it's such a good thing, why are you so depressed?"

Ben scowled. "Just look at me. I'm a mess. I know I shouldn't care, but I'm hideous." He rolled up both of his pants legs to emphasize his point. "I want to puke every time I see my lower legs. You don't know what it's like to be repulsed by your own body. If I can't look at myself, how can I ever expect Cassandra or any woman to look at me?"

Bruce tried to object, but Ben was on a roll.

"After that last scare, I might never again get plastic surgery to make my legs look better. I'm too afraid of what might happen. I can't take any more pain. I'm through with it. I can't stand it! I'm going to be grotesque for the rest of my life!"

Bruce burst out laughing.

"What's so funny?" demanded Ben.

"You are. Do you have any idea how crazy you sound? You're a living, breathing miracle. Do you have any idea how attractive that is to women? The thing is, women won't stay that way for long if you're not right with yourself. You've got to love yourself and your legs before you can expect anyone else to love you. It's self-responsibility. You and you alone are responsible for the way you feel. If you put it on someone else to love you first, or see yourself through their eyes, it's a cop out. You can't place your happiness on what someone else thinks of you. It has to come from within."

Ben silently considered what Bruce was saying.

"Look inside yourself and you'll see there is a wonderful, strong, perseverant, bull-headed…"

"Okay, okay, I get your point," sighed Ben.

"Do you? Because I'm not sure you really do. These legs of yours are special. They're better than bionic. When you've been down, they've carried you time and time again, first on the football field, then to win the American Cancer Society one mile race. But how many times have you ever stopped to appreciate them? How many times have you nearly lost them since the accident and they've still carried you through?"

Bruce's voice rose to emphasize his point. "They refuse to give up on you, but where's your gratitude for them? All you do is throw hate back their way. There's nothing positive about it. If you want them to work for you, be healthy for you, do what you need them to, then show them the love they deserve. You've got to love your legs. Love them with everything you've got. They are your best friends and they will never do you wrong if you treat them right."

Ben stared at Bruce. He'd never thought about his legs that way. "You're right," he said quietly. "It's time I showed them a little gratitude."

* * *

"I have a surprise for you," said Cassandra with a wide smile.

"Mmm, what is it?" asked Ben breathing in her perfume. She looked stunning in a forest green cocktail dress that perfectly matched her eyes. It was New Year's Eve and they'd made plans to drive to his college and surprise his fraternity brothers at a huge party they were throwing.

"Are your eyes really closed?" she asked leaning in to test his vision.

"Yes, they're really closed."

"Ok, hold out your hand," she said placing something long and cold in it.

Ben opened his eyes. "You got me a cane?" he asked incredulously.

"Look," she said shaking the sparkly tassels, "it's all decked out for New Years, horn and everything!"

"Thanks," he said flatly. "Now you can take your crippled boyfriend out in style."

Cassandra's face fell. "You don't like it."

"No, not really."

"I guess I shouldn't have bothered," she said in a hurt voice.

"No, you shouldn't have," he spat back.

"You don't have to be a jerk about it. I was just trying to show my support and do something nice."

"Never mind, you don't get it."

"Get what, Ben? That you're acting rude?"

"Maybe you should have thought before giving me such a thoughtless gift!"

"I'll have you know I went to four different shops and paid good money for my 'thoughtless gift,' and then I spent all afternoon finding the perfect decorations for it. So you're right, I'm completely thoughtless!" Cassandra fumed. "What's your excuse for being a Class A jerk?"

Ben shook his head, "Let's just go."

"Good idea, I can see this is going to be a fun-filled night."

"It will as long as I don't have to take that stupid cane."

"What's your problem?"

"My problem is I don't want it!"

"Fine, I'll take it back and get you a different one."

"I don't want that cane or any cane. My goal isn't to have a fancier or more stylish stick."

"But you need one right now. I was just trying to help you make the best of it."

"I don't want to make the best of it. I want to walk completely on my own like any normal person."

Cassandra snorted.

"What's that supposed to mean?" asked Ben, eyes still blazing.

"You've never been normal. Not even before the accident!"

Ben smiled. "Thanks a lot," he said drawing her into his embrace. "What do you say we get to that New Year's Eve party?"

While driving to the party, Ben realized that Cassandra was only trying to raise his spirits when she bought him the cane. "I'm sorry for being cranky," he said.

"I should be over it by next year," she joked, while affectionately touching his hand.

* * *

Ben lived at home that final semester and commuted to school when needed. The academic environment and commitment to his studies was therapeutic. As an extra bonus, there was a mild improvement in his reading level as well as his short-term memory and other cognitive skills. He was now able to comprehend books and literature after reading them two or three times. Plus, he finally fulfilled one of his most significant post-accident goals. He was walking without a cane. Even though he felt very unsteady at times, being able to walk unassisted made him glow with excitement. He was certain that the emotional high he experienced while walking would never go away.

Because he had more free time and his confidence was returning, he socialized more, which made him feel increasingly normal.

"Have you given any thought to the All-Male Revue?" asked Jack as they walked to class early that spring.

"No. Why?" Ben asked.

"Oh, I don't know, because we should MC it again."

Ben stopped and starred at Jack. "I don't know."

"Come on, it will be fun like old times."

Though Ben had regained much of his upper body bulk through weightlifting, and knew he could balance well enough to dance, he was still incredibly self-conscious.

"You know how I feel about letting people see my legs."

"So your voice still works, just MC and don't dance at the end."

Ben shook his head. "No way. Too many people will ask questions. Besides, you know how it is. Once you're on stage, the women will start screaming and demanding I take my clothes off. I'll never make it out of there alive."

Jack laughed. "You're right about that. But what if you could have it both ways?"

"What are you talking about?"

"What if you could strip, but not show anything?"

Ben laughed. "Yeah right."

"What do you think fan dancers do?"

"I'm not fan dancing."

"No, but they create the illusion of taking it all off, while keeping things strategically covered. We could do the same thing."

"I'm listening."

"What if we both wore red bandannas around our lower legs as part of our act? No one would be able to see your scars and I'll wrap up mine too. No one will ever suspect we're wearing them to cover your scars."

"Sounds great. But I still don't see how we're going to pull it off."

"Just trust me. I've got the perfect plan."

For the next few weeks, Ben and Jack practiced their routine in Jack's apartment. They worked so hard, Ben heard the music in his head. It followed him everywhere. By the night of the show, he was confident he could pull the routine off in style.

Jack and Ben took turns introducing the acts from cowboys to firefighters and everything in between. While some of the acts were steamy, most were just plain funny. Ben hadn't laughed so hard in months.

As the evening drew to a close, the women began to yell for Jack and Ben to perform.

"Should we do it?" Jack said loudly into his mic.

"I don't know if they can handle it," Ben shouted above the screaming women.

"Sounds like they're willing to risk it," laughed Jack.

"It is for charity," agreed Ben. "All right hit it."

The speakers behind them crackled to life and Wild Cherry's *Play that Funky Music* came on.

The crowd went crazy as Ben and Jack stripped to their Skivvies!

* * *

As the horns blasted the unending loop of Pomp and Circumstance, Ben's heart nearly burst with pride. Not only was he graduating, he was walking down the aisle without a cane!

Applause broke as his family spotted him and cheered wildly.

"That's our boy!" shouted Hank pounding his giant hands together.

"We love you Ben!" yelled Doris.

Ben's eyes welled with tears as he made his way to the front row. He nonchalantly wiped them with his palm. What a road it had been. Visions of the past year and a half flashed through his head, being on MTV, wearing Ace's prized shirt, demonstrating the *100 Ways to Pick up Women*, waking up in the hospital, learning to walk, talking with Art, implementing Coach Mainieri's rule, coming home, returning to school, the 15 surgeries and the plastic surgery scare. He had become a different person. Though he wouldn't wish his accident on anyone, he also wouldn't trade the experiences it had brought him. He knew in his heart that he was a much better, kinder, and more compassionate person for it.

The student sitting next to Ben nudged him. "They're calling you."

Ben stood just in time to hear the announcer say, "Graduating Magna Cum Laude, with high honors, Ben Nevets."

CHAPTER THIRTY-TWO

RUNNING

Ben stood at the head of his parents' long driveway. Trees and plants lined the expansive stretch of pavement giving him the privacy he needed. He knew he looked ridiculous in his running shorts with ace bandages all the way up to his knees. Though he didn't need the coverings, he was so embarrassed by his scars that he didn't want anyone to see them. As if that wasn't bad enough, he was about to make a royal spectacle of himself. One year after learning to walk, he was determined to run again too.

He walked a few feet, surveying his surroundings. Except for the slight grade, which couldn't even really be considered a hill, it was perfect. He breathed in and out listening to the sound of his breath in his head. Ben then reflected as to whether he was making a mistake by not following his doctors' advice.

"You should feel lucky that you can walk at all," Ben's doctor said when Ben asked about the possibility of running again.

"But I can walk, so why can't I run again?"

"It's not that simple," the doctor had explained. "We don't know the full impact of what's happened to your brain. We already know your injury impacted your ability to balance."

"Yes, but I've worked that out. I'm fine now."

"Walking yes, but it's a slower paced skill, giving you more time to compensate for any missteps. Then there's the portion of the brain that handles issues of speed and coordination. Yours was seriously damaged."

"But I'll never know until I try."

"It's not healthy to get your hopes up like this. You've come extremely far, but even you have limits. The chances of being able to run with the injuries you sustained are very slim."

Ben had gotten a second and third opinion on the matter. Every doctor had had similar answers. But that wasn't going to stop him.

He'd asked for hints and tips on how to start running anyway, but no one was either willing or able to give him advice. He was on his own again.

"You can do this," he said, envisioning himself running along the long driveway. He clumsily tried to throw one leg out in front of the other, but it barely moved. It was painful, awkward, and scary. No matter how he tried to start, he couldn't quite get himself to run. He wanted to, he really wanted to, yet his body had forgotten how to do it. Making things even more difficult, his muscles were still atrophied and his joints were extremely stiff. He walked in circles trying to figure it out how he'd ever run. It had always been so easy before.

"I don't get it," he said aloud. "It's just quickly putting one foot in front of the other, walking only faster."

He stopped. That's it, he thought. I'll just practice walking really fast first. The technique proved to be more effective than trying to run from a dead standstill.

Soon Ben was speed walking down the driveway. Gradually, he lifted his forward knee higher and followed through with his other knee to give the appearance of running. He wasn't concerned with speed, just helping his body memorize what running felt like. He was surprised at how difficult it was to coordinate his legs to move in back and forth strides.

At first Ben could only take five or six awkward strides. Most people who saw him would not have guessed he was trying to run. He looked more like a kid amusing himself with weird walking techniques. But he continued to practice several times a day. With continued work, five feet became ten feet, then twenty feet, then twenty yards. After a few months, he was able to jog. In time, he was running around the block.

Running and the aftermath at times were extremely painful, but it didn't matter. Ben was just happy to be able to run again. He had accomplished yet another thing that his doctors told him was not possible.

To celebrate his success and help him always remember what he had regained, Ben decided to run several times a week for the rest of his life. He hoped that if he kept it up, his running abilities would eventually match his pre-accident levels.

CHAPTER THIRTY-THREE

LAW SCHOOL

Bridgeport, Connecticut, September

The first year of law school, to virtually all students, is the most intellectually challenging and humbling experience of their lives. The kinds of people who attend law school are typically type-A overachievers, who usually graduated at the top of their respective colleges and universities. Law professors waste no time deflating such egos and shattering the over-confident. Ben had seen movies and read books about the cutthroat first year. Because success in law school is based on individual class rank, students are extremely competitive and get pleasure from their peers' failure.

Ben had no illusions about what he was getting himself into. He had a much less impressive background than the other students. The fact that he had the unique honor of probably being the only law student in history to have severe brain damage did little to comfort him, though he thought in a way it might give him an edge. His ego had already been knocked down to size about a hundred times over since the accident.

Ben had no idea how he was going to last for more than a few weeks in law school. He wasn't even sure he really wanted to be a lawyer anymore. It was more that he couldn't let down his friends and family. He was too embarrassed to tell them he didn't think he could make it. He was even more embarrassed and afraid of the day he would have to admit that his accident and brain damage caused him to fail. He was sure that failing would be like a scarlet letter he would have to wear for the rest of his life, no matter what he did or how successful he became.

The night before he'd left for school, his mother brought up one of her favorite childhood stories about Ben. He didn't even remember it, but his mother was so fond of telling it that he knew it by heart.

"You were 13 and it was just before your bar mitzvah."

"Yes, Mom," Ben smiled affectionately at her.

"The school paper interviewed you and asked what you wanted to be when you grew up. And what did you say?"

"A lawyer?" Ben answered.

"Actually, you wrote that you wanted to be a 'famous lawyer.'"

"Really? A famous lawyer?"

"I had no idea that's what you wanted, but now here you are," she said with tears in her eyes. "My baby, all grown up. To think we almost lost you."

She gave him a kiss and looked at him with such pride that he couldn't bear to disappoint her. He just didn't have any idea how he was going to pull it off. After considering his options for the hundredth time, he made himself a deal. He would go to law school, but remain open to dropping out if it became too difficult to manage. He would just tell everyone that he realized that the law wasn't for him. Of course, Ben didn't share the decision with his family. It was best not to worry them until he knew for certain what he was going to do.

He shared a house with a few other law students whom he'd met during orientation. Although he shared the story of his accident with them, he didn't go into great detail about his injuries and he certainly didn't mention that he had brain damage. Instead, he tried very hard to hide the overwhelming insecurity and problems that went along with it with his many cognitive deficits.

When classes began, he hoped the professors would gradually present the coursework to ease the transition. Unfortunately, the transition was limited to less than a minute of an introduction, followed by getting right into the intense subject matter.

He soon learned his professors were fond of the "Socratic Method." It involved the professor starting a dialog with a random student, followed by drilling with in-depth questions about the subject matter and reasoning of a particular case or law.

It scared the crap out of most law students. In fact, Ben had heard horror stories about students who'd had nervous breakdowns because of the method.

Not only did Ben have a very hard time understanding and following the professors throughout the classes he attended, he sat in fear that he would be the student selected to debate the professor. He also feared that his responses would immediately alert the students and professors of his cognitive disabilities.

Worst of all, when Ben attempted the daily assigned reading, it was as if he was reading a foreign language.

Ben decided to approach the challenges of the first year of law school the same way he'd approached football and the accident rehabilitation. Just as he pushed himself to try twice as hard when his body felt like giving up in the past, he used the desire to quit law school as an incentive to try twice as hard to continue studying.

Between classes, when his peers chatted or grabbed a bite to eat, he always went to the library to read assignments. After classes, he read until he went to sleep eight to ten hours later. Weekends, when other students were doing various social activities, Ben would mostly read and study the course materials.

The amount of time he put in would have given any other student a sizable advantage over their peers. But for Ben, the added hours were barely enough to even keep up and comprehend what he was reading.

"Hi Dad," Ben greeted his father in a phone call after a particularly trying day of classes.

"Hi Ben. You sound down."

"I don't know if I can do it."

"Don't know if you can do what, Ben?"

"Law school. I spend every waking minute reading and I don't think it's enough. It's like studying in a foreign country. I don't understand the language."

"You mean the Latin terms?"

"I mean all of it."

"Today, Professor Tremble called on me to answer a question from last night's reading assignment and I didn't have the slightest idea what he was talking about. I don't know if I haven't read it yet, or if I did and just don't remember. Either way, he really let me have it. It was humiliating to be singled out."

"Have you told any of the professors about your accident?"

"I don't think it would make a difference here. It's so vicious here. I don't want to prejudice them before they get to know me…or give them any more ammunition against me. Besides, even if a professor was compassionate about my setbacks, grading is anonymous here and in most law schools, so they don't know whose test is whose."

Hank strained to hear as Ben exhaled softly. There was a catch in his son's voice that made him wonder if Ben was holding back tears.

"Ben, it would be all right to drop out, if that's what you want."

"I don't want to quit," Ben said a little too quickly.

"You don't have to torture yourself or prove anything to anyone. You're already a hero in my book."

"Dad," Ben admonished in the tone used for family when they make biased claims.

"I just don't want you to think becoming an attorney is the end all be all. I have plenty of clients who are attorneys. Do you have any idea how many of them are happy with their career choice?"

"Most of them," answered Ben.

"None of them."

"Come on, Dad," Ben laughed.

"Ok, maybe not all of them. But I guarantee you, plenty of the attorneys I help are very unhappy people and much of that unhappiness stems from their choice of careers."

"If that's really true, why haven't you tried to stop me before?"

"All I'm saying is that I love you and hate to see you going through any more pain or hardship unnecessarily. Don't do this just to please us."

"We want you to be happy," said Doris picking up the extension. "If you're not happy, you can come home at any time. There are hundreds of things a smart guy like you could do with his life."

"Thanks Mom, but I think I'll stay a while longer. We need a good attorney in the family."

"If that's what you want. But don't do it for us. We love you no matter what."

Ben thought about quitting every day. Every time he drove to class, he considered not taking the next exit, calling it quits, and driving home to his parents. It would have been so easy to travel the extra hour south and give up. But he wasn't a quitter, so he continued to stay in the moment, taking each day one day at a time. When his housemates discussed class topics, he tried very hard to listen without participating in the conversations. He hoped he might glean new insight from listening, but didn't want them to know how overwhelmingly difficult law school was for him.

A few days became a few weeks and then a few months and he was still there. Though the majority of time was devoted to work, he allowed himself breaks when Cassandra, or other friends, came to visit on the weekends. Occasionally, he'd go out to dinner or a bar with his housemates.

For the most part, he was able to avoid being called on in class by keeping his head down and trying to blend into the background of the class. He was convinced most professors delighted in humiliating students who were not prepared.

Late in the semester, Ben made the mistake of getting to Murphy's class minutes after it began. He could have kicked himself for oversleeping. With all the good seats taken, his only choice was to sit in the very last row, which almost assured he'd be called on.

Ben sank low in his seat and tried to follow Murphy's line of reasoning. But soon he realized that he was completely lost. He twisted to see the large industrial clock on the wall behind him. There was still more than an hour to go. He had no idea how he was going to survive. He'd read the assigned reading, but couldn't remember any of it or how it remotely applied to the class discussion. His mind raced as he tried to latch on to any meaningful word or phrase to help him understand the complicated intellectual topic.

Murphy paced as he shot questions at students as if he were firing a machine gun. Ben sank lower in his seat, wishing he could become invisible. One by one, the humiliated students fell by the wayside.

Ben forced himself to concentrate even harder, but it was no use. Professor Murphy might as well have been speaking Chinese. He caught sight of a watch on student in front of him. Forty-five minutes to go. He could swear time was slowing down just to spite him.

Ben checked his notes from the previous class, then opened his book to the assigned reading, but none of it seemed to apply. He desperately scanned the desks of others to see if anyone had their textbook open to the right page, but everyone seemed to be on different pages. He twisted again, to look at the clock behind him. Less than 20 minutes. He took a deep breath. He might just be able to make it.

With five minutes left until the end of class, suddenly Ben became aware that everyone around him was staring in his direction.

"We're waiting, Ben…" demanded Professor Murphy.

Ben ran a hand through his hair as his mind raced. It figured, just when he thought he might be out of the woods, he was caught. Shaking his head at the irony he said aloud, "Murphy's Law."

The class burst out laughing and several people clapped him on the back.

"Touché," laughed Professor Murphy at Ben's unintended pun. "I couldn't have summarized the issue's complexity better myself."

Ben grinned, pleased to take the credit, even though he still had no idea what Murphy had been discussing.

Because the students weren't tested until the end of the semester, there was no way for Ben to fail until December. He stuck closely to his study regimen, reading between classes, after dinner until bed each night. He felt like he was reading every waking moment of his existence.

Surprisingly, something was happening. The more he studied, the easier it got. Soon he was reading paragraphs only three times, then just twice, until he was reading things just once like everyone else! He was also reading faster than he used to. Soon the cognitive deficits began to fall away too. One by one, he shed the attention issues and vocabulary obstacles that had plagued him. Memories came together and he no longer had difficulty associating stories with the proper person. He rarely repeated himself and his sense of direction sharpened tremendously. It was as if his complex, disoriented mind was snapping back together.

With so many dramatic cognitive changes, time flew by. The first set of exams came quicker then Ben anticipated. On the one hand, he was glad he hadn't been tested throughout the semester. On the other hand, he hadn't studied or taken an exam since before the accident, which felt like 10 lifetimes ago. How would he do? Would the tests prove that all his restored cognitive abilities were just figments of his imagination? Part of him was afraid to know the answer.

Virtually all of the students worked with study groups to prepare for the exams. But Ben was too insecure about his limitations and didn't want the other students to notice. Instead, he prepared by not only studying the text books, but also by purchasing and studying the concise summaries of the textbooks. The smaller books gave simpler perspectives than the entire textbook, similar to Cliff Notes.

With stubborn doggedness, he studied the textbooks and the summary books making outlines, reviewing each section, and quizzing himself. Despite feeling that his cognitive skills had improved dramatically, Ben didn't trust himself. He was sure his brain damage precluded him from relying on innate intelligence. All he could do was rely on very hard work.

It seemed to Ben that all the other students had a better grasp of their studies and were more prepared for the finals than he was. He was proud that he'd made it that far, but the four months he had attended law school would be meaningless if he failed the exams and flunked out.

After each exam, he walked out of the classroom certain he had failed. Instead of focusing on how poorly he did, he pushed on, completing five finals in two weeks. Relieved that he had lived through the first semester of law school and completed all the exams, he returned to his parents' home for the month-long winter break.

"How do you think you did?" asked Bruce when they were alone.

Ben smiled. "I don't have any regrets. I gave it my all."

"Then you think you passed?"

Ben laughed. "I doubt it. But I did my best."

Bruce shook his head. "We don't really need a lawyer in the family. You and I could always go into business together."

"Yeah right." Ben bit his lip. "What if I really did fail?"

Bruce shrugged. "Do you really think you did?"

"Maybe I should have just quit while I was ahead. It would have been less embarrassing to be the guy who never started law school, than to be the one who failed out of law school."

"Give yourself a break. You've had some pretty serious injuries. So what if you're not the world's smartest guy?"

"But that's just it. If I hadn't had the accident, I would have done much better. I know I would have. Now my legal career is about to fall off a cliff before it even takes off."

"Hold on, you don't know that."

"Don't I?" said Ben pacing the length of his bedroom. "And the worst part is I was making so much progress," he said stopping to face his brother. "I honestly think the reason my mind has improved so much in the past four months is because I've been studying so hard. I'm like an athlete in training. I grow stronger every day that I practice. But if I fail law school, I don't have any reason to practice any more. It's all going to stop."

"Sounds to me like you have a great reason to practice no matter what happens."

Ben's eyes raked across his brother's face as if somehow Bruce could give him the answer he was searching for. "But what will I do? What am I supposed to study?"

"What is that Dad is always telling us? Stay in the moment?"

"But..."

"But all your buts are just what ifs. Nothing has come to pass yet. It's time to stay in the moment and see what happens. If you don't pass, then it's time to decide what to do next. And you know we'll all be more than willing to make suggestions."

Ben returned to law school in mid-January. Even though he didn't have his grades from the first semester, he felt more confident and comfortable with his classes than when he started law school last September. He now knew many of the students and several of the professors. Plus, he had a good idea of what to expect and how to handle his studies.

Three weeks into the second semester, grades were posted. No names were listed next to the scores, just personal identification numbers, but the thought of his marks out there for the whole world to read made Ben nervous.

"They're here!" shouted George, one of Ben's housemates. Everyone knew exactly what he meant. Soon doors were opening and shutting all over the house as the rest of the group gathered to hear what George had to say.

He stood in the front hall, pink cheeked and panting, as if he'd run the entire ten miles from campus through the frozen Connecticut winter.

"They're all up, Louis, Murphy, Tremble, Castro, you name it, they've posted."

"Is it bad?" asked Neil, another one of Ben's housemates.

"There are a bunch of Ds and Fs. So much for thinking that law schools collect too much in tuition to fail their students out of school." George's eyes sparkled with delight to be the center of attention.

"There really are a bunch of Ds and Fs?" Ben echoed breathlessly. "That means some students don't have a chance regardless of their grades second semester. You can't be serious."

"I agree. I just hope it's not Nicole. She's a hottie," said George. Then he said solemnly. "I about had a heart attack when I started looking down Castro's sheet. Not one person above me passed. I was sure I was dead. But I pulled it…" George's voice trailed off as Ben ran out the door.

He didn't even realize he'd forgotten his coat until he was roaring down the street in his car. Though he could see his icy breath in the air, he was sweating. This was it. The moment of truth was upon him. Though he didn't have class until tomorrow, there was no way he'd wait another second to learn his destiny. He'd waited almost two years for this.

His mind raced. How was he going to tell his roommates he was one of the ones who'd failed? How could he break it to his family, Cassandra, his fraternity brothers?

The walk from the parking lot to the school usually seemed agonizingly long, but Ben barely noticed it. Inside, a large group of students stood clustered around the life-changing documents. The pit of his stomach burned and butterflies danced up his spine as he squeezed through the throng of anxious students. He slowly ran his finger down the list, embarrassed to let others see his grades and yet afraid that his eyes wouldn't match the correct student ID number with the correct scores.

He paused when his finger hit his number and ran it across. His heart skipped a beat. He had a few Cs, a B-, and a D+. He ran his finger across again to double check. The grades were still there.

"C average." A slow smile spread across his face. "C is for cookie, that's good enough for me," he laughed quoting a Cookie Monster song. He hummed a few bars of the tune, not caring how crazy he sounded. He had passed his first semester with a C average, enough to stay in law school!

Under normal pre-accident circumstances, he wouldn't have been happy with the scores, but it meant he was still in law school. Not to mention, the average grades meant that he had done better than at least a quarter of his class, and none of them had brain damage!

The second semester of law school was more difficult than the first. But Ben continued to put in the same amount of time into studying. On March 20th Ben called Doris.

"Good morning Mom, do you know what day it is?"

"Wednesday?"

Ben laughed, "No, it's my second birthday!"

Doris shuddered. She'd tried so hard to forget the anniversary of Ben's accident. "Oh, I forgot."

"Come on Mom, it's a day to celebrate. I'm alive!"

"Oh Ben, I don't know why you want to remember such a horrible day."

"Because, it's when I became who I am today. If it weren't for my accident, I wouldn't appreciate the world half as much as I do now. I wouldn't know what it takes to walk, or appreciate how much effort it takes to learn new things. And I probably wouldn't understand the true meaning of staying in the moment."

She supposed he was right. But she still wished to forget the living nightmare. She didn't want to think about how scared she'd been or the tubes and wires running out of him while he lay so perfectly still.

"Perhaps we can agree to each commemorate this day in our own way. You by celebrating and me forgetting it ever happened."

"All right Mom," laughed Ben. He could see it still bothered her. "I just wanted to thank you again and tell you how much I love you for being there when I needed you most."

Doris smiled into the phone. "Ben, you never have to thank me for doing what a mother is supposed to do."

As it was nearing the end of the second semester, Ben was certain that he had overcome all of his post-accident cognitive deficits. Still, he wanted more proof that he was "cured."

As his peers were excited to spend their summer on the beach, or for internships at law firms, Ben was excited to be examined by a neuropsychologist.

Dr. Michael Morris was a well-respected neuropsychologist who specialized in interpreting the impact brain injuries had on the cognition of survivors.

"It's been two years since your accident," said Dr. Morris. "Why are you coming to me now?"

"Because, I've had improvements," smiled Ben. "Dramatic improvements. So much so, that I believe that I am actually ahead of where I was before my traumatic brain injury. I need someone to tell me I'm not crazy. That these things can happen, are real, and not my mind playing tricks on me."

Dr. Morris gave Ben a fatherly pat. "You need to realize that you had a severe traumatic brain injury as a result of your accident. People with your type of injury, although they can improve, it's typically not anything near their pre-accident levels."

A little voice inside Ben's head remembered, "Touch the brain, never the same," over and over again. He shook his head to push it aside. "I know that's what neuro-doctors say, but I have," Ben insisted. "I swear I feel like my old self again. I can perform just as well; in fact I'm feeling smarter than I did before the accident."

The doctor took a deep breath. "Why is this so important to you? If you feel good, shouldn't that be enough?"

"I know it should, but I need proof."

"And if I can't give you that proof, what will happen then?"

Ben swallowed hard. "Then at least I'll know."

The test took more than six hours. Some portions of the exam were very easy, while others were quite difficult. It consisted of everything from oral questions to questions about patterns and logic. Some portions of the exam were very obscure. Ben had no idea how it tested his intelligence. For example, he was shown four different shapes and asked to pick the most likely fifth shape.

By the end of the test, Ben's head was a whirl of numbers, shapes, and letters. So many of the questions seemed rather strange. By that point, he was so doubtful of his abilities that he thought of telling the doctor to forget about completing the analysis. Maybe the doctor was right. Maybe he hadn't improved as much as he had thought.

A few weeks later, he met with Dr. Morris to go over the test results.

"I've never seen anything like it," said the shocked neuropsychologist. "I've run through the tests three times and every time they've come back the same. You perform at a much higher level than average people in your age group."

"You mean people with my kind of brain injuries?" asked Ben.

"I mean any kind of people," smiled Dr. Morris.

"Then my brain damage is gone?"

"No, you still have brain damage. You always will have brain scars, but the brain is a strange and mysterious thing. It can compensate for a lot, teach itself to work in new and different ways. It appears that's exactly what you've done."

"So what does that mean?"

"It means that you have a very positive future. You are as mentally capable as anyone else out there."

"And it's not going to disappear?"

"Why should it? You've created new pathways in your brain."

That summer, Ben received his second semester grades and his overall average and class rank for the first year. To Ben's delight, he received all Bs and one C+. His first-year grades actually ranked him in the top half of his class.

It was then Ben knew that he was definitely going to become a lawyer one day. Nothing would stop him. Reaching that goal had less to do with wanting to work in the profession, and much more to do with officially overcoming all his accident-related problems. If he could do that, he knew that he could do anything if he was willing to pay the price and work very hard.

* * *

There was one more thing Ben had to do before he could go back to school that fall. He wanted to go back to where his life had changed forever. He had to go see where the accident had happened.

"It just looks like a regular street," said Ben in amazement as he stared down Ocean Avenue.

"Of course, what did you think it would look like?" asked his girlfriend.

He shrugged. "I don't know, different somehow. My life was turned upside down here. I nearly died close to this spot, yet it's as if nothing ever happened here."

She gently touched his back. "The only thing constant in life is change."

Ben nodded. "I know, but what's difficult to wrap my brain around is that the accident was so big and life changing, yet there's no evidence here that it ever took place."

"Maybe the place doesn't matter so much, because the real change wasn't to it, but to you."

"How did you get so smart?" he asked taking her into his arms. In the process of nuzzling her something caught his eye. "Oh my G-d!"

"What is it?"

"I think it's the Big's Beachside Bar!" he said pointing to a sign in the distance.

She squinted. "What's Big's Beachside Bar?"

"It's the bar Johnnie drank at!"

Her eyes widened. "You mean the drunk driver?"

"Yes. I'm certain," said Ben. "You know what; I've got to see this guy with my own eyes. Tonight, while you're in the hotel, I'm going to check this place out."

That night when Ben walked into the bar, a burst of cold air hit them in the face as Ben flung open the door.

"Easy there," said a bouncer. "Can I help you with something?"

Ben looked around the sporty club and waited for his eyes to adjust. "Maybe you could help me," he improvised. "I'm looking for a friend of mine; he drinks here every now and then. His name is Johnnie Sconner."

"Johnnie? He's still working, right over there."

Ben nearly choked at the irony, but quickly turned it into a cough. "Thanks man," he said staring towards the bartender. His heart was racing.

Hank had always told him that the drunk driver didn't deserve one ounce of their attention, so Ben had tried not to think about him. When he had, he'd always envisioned some sloppy, unshaven, slob. He'd always assumed the guy couldn't stand up straight, probably slurred his words, and smelled awful like something dragged out of a sewer. But the guy working behind the counter was none of those things. This guy was a clean-cut, regular-looking guy, not much older than himself. He joked with fellow employees as he walked back and forth tending to his customers and mixing drinks.

Ben watched in disbelief. The hair on the back of Ben's neck stood on end. How could Johnnie be working for the same bar he got drunk at the night of my accident? Why did everyone let him drive drunk? How many times had they let him go out into the night since the accident to hurt other people? Didn't the owners care? Didn't he care what he was doing to people, that he was ruining lives?

Ben turned around and headed back to his hotel where his girlfriend was waiting.

"Did you tell him who you are?" she asked.

"No."

"Why not?"

Ben shrugged. "Because I don't want him to see me the way I look now. According to my fraternity brothers, seeing me that night lying on the street still keeps them awake at nights. If Johnnie ever thinks about the accident, I want him to remember me broken in a pool of blood. I want him to think about all the pain, suffering and hardship he's caused. I hope he has nightmares about what he's done. I hope he lies awake wondering whatever happened to me. I hope he gets to feel a tenth of the pain I've felt. And if he does, even that would be too good for him."

CHAPTER THIRTY-FOUR

PERFECT MATCH

That fall, Ben returned to law school with renewed confidence. He'd found much of the closure he'd been seeking. Even though he'd been given a clean bill of mental health, he was more determined than ever to become a model student. He didn't settle for being as good as he had been before the accident; he wanted to be an even better reader, more complex conversationalist, and formidable debater. To his great surprise, even though the classes were more complicated, his grades dramatically improved, and the work became more manageable.

It was as though giving him a clean bill of mental health had removed an invisible barrier that held him back. Now that he knew he was "the same as everyone else," he was free to take on the world without limitations.

Though Ben's walking and running dramatically improved, his legs would occasionally have a "hiccup," causing him to lose coordination and trip. In most cases, he never actually fell, just stumbled and missed a step. When it happened he would become embarrassed, but learned to not make a big deal of it and just keep walking.

On an early spring night during Ben's second year of law school, he and George headed out to their favorite bar. George was the designated driver, so Ben was looking forward to having a couple of drinks.

"It always surprises me that you don't have any problem with alcohol after what happened to you," commented George as they pulled into the pub.

"Why should it? I enjoy a beer just as much as the next guy," said Ben hopping out of the car.

"You aren't worried about the evils of alcohol and all that?" asked George only half kidding.

Ben shook his head. "There's no such thing. It's just a drink like any other when people are responsible. It's when they do stupid things like drink and drive, that's when I have a problem."

The two went inside and began mingling. Toward the end of the night, Ben tripped as he walked through the crowd.

"Did you just get those legs?" asked a beautiful blonde.

Ben frowned. "You shouldn't say things like that. I was in a serious accident three years ago and had to learn how to walk again."

The blonde pouted her lips and pretended to play the violin. "Nice try Romeo. Do girls actually fall for that line?"

Ben wasn't used to such a reaction. Whenever he told his story, women usually fell all over him with great interest and sympathy. But this woman was different. He knew in an instant that he liked her.

"I'm Ben. What's your name?"

"Dawn."

"Listen Dawn, my buddy and I were just about to take off. It was nice meeting you."

"Don't you want my number? Better yet, why don't you give me your number?" She fished in her purse and withdrew a Sharpie, which she handed to Ben. Then she handed him a notebook.

* * *

That night, Dawn rummaged through her purse. "Crap, it's gone!"

"What?" asked Kristine.

"My notebook."

Kristine shrugged, "There can't be much in it. Get a new one."

Dawn looked all over her apartment for the notebook. "You don't understand, this guy gave me his number tonight."

Kristine laughed, "You get numbers all the time, what makes this one so special?"

"I don't know, he was kind of cute and really funny. Damn it, it's not here!"

"Forget about him, I'm sure the notebook's long gone."

Dawn bit her lip. "I've got to go back."

Kristine checked her watch. "Do you have any idea what time it is? The bar's been closed for at least fifteen minutes."

"I'm heading back to the bar."

"Are you crazy? Wait till morning."

Dawn shook her head. "I've gotta do it now. It might not be there if I wait."

"It probably won't be there now," said Kristine rolling her eyes as Dawn rushed out the door.

Just as Kristine predicted, the parking lot was empty. A single street-light flickered, its weak bulb threatening to go out at any moment. Dawn jumped out of the car and looked all over the parking lot.

Dawn began walking the parking lot trying to remember where she'd parked.

"Bingo!" thought Dawn running toward something fluttering in the breeze.

She flipped through the damp pages. "It's still here!"

Chapter Thirty-Five

THE BAR

Ben kept up his rigorous study regimen despite the positive prognosis from Dr. Morris. Even though he'd been told that he wouldn't slip backwards, a part him feared that he would. He was living a dream that seemed too good to be true and he never wanted to take it for granted. And so he spent every evening studying until bedtime.

He was so immersed in *The Nature of the Judicial Process*, that he nearly hit the ceiling when the phone rang.

It had sounded like a gun blast in the stillness of his room and it took him a moment to realize what it was. He scanned the room for the source of the ringing and located the white plastic coils of the cord sticking out from under a pile of folders on the floor.

"Hello?" he answered.

"So I was wondering," said a seductive voice. "You never did tell me how old you are."

"Dawn? Is that you?"

"Yes. Are you avoiding the question?" she teased.

"Not at all. I'm 35," he joked back.

The line went quiet as she tried to figure out if he was serious.

"Dawn?"

Still no answer.

"Dawn, I was joking. I'm only 24."

"Smartass," she said in a relieved voice.

"So how old are you?"

"Don't you know a lady never reveals her age?"

Ben smiled. He really liked her playful nature and the way she constantly kept him on his toes.

"So would you like to go out sometime?" he asked.

"Sure, I'd love to go out sometime soon."

Ben and Dawn hit it off and began seeing each other regularly. As Ben got to know her more, he realized he was no longer interested in his arrangement with Cassandra to see other people. Part of him felt very guilty, but they'd been growing further apart since the end of his first year of law school. He didn't even miss her when she wasn't around. Now, all he wanted to do was spend time with Dawn.

As it turned out, Dawn was an undergraduate at a nearby college, who worked part-time as a telephone operator for Saks Fifth Avenue. The more time Ben spent with Dawn, the more he adored her. Not only did she share his sense of humor and accept him for who he was, scars and all, she understood and supported his blooming legal ambitions.

When Ben finally graduated from law school a year and a half later, he was ranked in the top half of his class. It was only then that Ben realized he'd worked so hard on getting through law school that he lacked the experience of most of his peers. He'd never had an internship at a law firm. Although he had briefly volunteered working at a county law office, the reality was that all he had to put on his resume were his pre-accident accomplishments and summer jobs. With little else to include in the way of job experience, he was left with no choice but to list his employment and experience as a lifeguard and swim instructor.

Law clerking was the most ideal first job for most graduating law students. It involved working side by side with a superior court judge for one year. It is said that the lessons learned during that year are so valuable to a starting attorney, that it sets a very strong foundation for their future legal career.

Ben really wanted a chance to become a law clerk back in New Jersey, but knew that he probably didn't have the qualifications or experience for the position.

"You should try anyway," Dawn encouraged.

"I don't know. I'm sure they get thousands of resumes."

"Then make yours a thousand and one."

"You don't understand, there are only 30 positions available in each county. It'd be like winning the lottery."

"Are you afraid of a little competition?"

"Yes. They all have so many more qualifications than I have."

Dawn shook her head. "After all you've been through, you still don't get it."

"Get what?"

"You may not have been the valedictorian of your class, or have had a fancy internship at a prestigious New York firm, but you are every bit as good as those other applicants. Your accomplishments are far greater than anything they've ever achieved. You're a success because you persevere when others give up. You know your abilities are limitless if you put your mind to it."

"I suppose you're right," he said hugging her.

She kissed his cheek. "I'm always right. Besides, the only thing you have to lose is the stamp to send it in. If they don't pick you, you're no worse off than you are right now."

And so Ben sent his resume to the Superior Court of New Jersey in hopes of securing a law clerk position after law school graduation.

In addition to finding a job, Ben needed to take the bar exams. Every bar candidate in the country was required to take a one-day, multi-state bar exam, along with a second day of exams for their particular state. Although most of his peers were taking these two exams, Ben decided to add a third. He figured if he was going to commit himself to the most intense studying months in his life, he might as well get the most bang for his buck. He decided to take both the New Jersey and the Pennsylvania bar exams. Both were scheduled for same week in July.

If he failed both New Jersey and Pennsylvania, then he would have failed anyway. If he passed New Jersey and failed Pennsylvania, then there would be little lost. If he was fortunate enough to pass both New Jersey and Pennsylvania, then he figured he would be in pretty good shape.

Just like he had so many times before, he set a rigorous study schedule for himself. He started every morning by taking a three-hour bar preparation course, which ended at 11:30 am. Then he went to the gym for an hour workout. The remainder of the day was spent studying. After dinner, he took portions of prior New Jersey and Multistate Bar exams. The late evening was spent on the phone or in person with Dawn. In the week prior to the exams, he did nothing but study alone for 15 hours per day.

By the time the exams arrived, Ben's mind had never been so challenged in all his life. He didn't think he'd ever held so much information in his brain at once. If he had been a computer, he was sure that his RAM drive would have been full.

His heart skipped a beat as he walked into the gigantic testing area. Thousands of individual desks filled a room the size of a football field. He shakily dropped into one of the seats nearest to him and pulled two No. 2 pencils out of his pocket.

The room filled rapidly as eager law students found their seats. Many went through pre-test rituals such as deep breathing, saying the rosary, or stretching. Ben tried to run through the questions from last night's study exam in his head. This first day was devoted to the required multi-state bar exam. Once the exam booklets and answer keys were handed out, the room went quiet...or so it seemed. As Ben tried to concentrate, he became acutely aware of the little noises around him. The guy next to him sounded like he had a deviated septum and was breathing in ragged, husky breaths, which reminded Ben of a phone stalker. Someone behind him kept coughing, while others shuffled papers, or scraped their chairs as they juggled for more comfortable positions. He tried to cover his ears as he worked, but the longer it went on, the louder it became and the more distracted he became.

As he answered each question, he reminded himself that he was one step closer to the end of the grueling tests and that one day it would simply be an unpleasant memory. Page after page, he answered questions that made his head spin. When he finally put the pencil down, he realized there were still 45 minutes left!

He looked around the big room and saw that everybody else was still intensely working. At first he was certain that he'd answered correctly, but then an overwhelming wave of panic washed over him. How could he have finished so far ahead of the others? He must have done something wrong. Maybe he hadn't read the instructions correctly.

He thought about rereading the test to make sure he was right. But then the image of his father crept into his mind. "Your first instinct is usually the correct one. Trust yourself." Ben took a deep breath and decided to go with his gut. Whatever the consequences, he would be fine.

The next day he brought a pair of earplugs with him. They proved to be very effective in drowning out the outside noise. The content of the bar exams proved to be quite similar to the practice tests that he'd taken.

At the end of the third day of testing, he turned a page and realized he was on the very last question.

After answering it, he put his pencil down. Relief washed over him. He had finished. No matter what the outcome, he had made it through, had no regrets, and he was proud of himself. He looked around the room. Nearly half the students were still writing. He wondered how many of them would have to come back and take the test again. Something in his gut twinged as he wondered if he would be one of them.

"No, I'm not going there," he told himself, "I won't second guess myself." He actually felt pretty good when he stopped to really think about it. He'd made it through all the exams and was sure that he'd given it his best.

He put the roof down on his black Celica convertible and cranked up the music.

Barry Manilow's *Daybreak* was playing.

He turned the volume up until the speakers vibrated.

It's time we let the spirit come in
Let it come on in
I'm singing to the world
Everybody's caught in the spin... Ben sang at the top of his lungs as he drove down the interstate. Life was truly good again! It would be months before the exam results were released. But he didn't care. He'd done what he set out to do.

If I don't pass, he thought, I'm not going to go through this again. I won't do this to myself ever again. I've proven my point. I will simply choose a different career. To reward himself, he took the month of August off and went on a week's vacation with Dawn.

When he arrived home, there was a letter from a superior court judge in Hackensack, New Jersey, inviting Ben to interview for one of the much sought-after law clerk positions.

"Congratulations," Doris said, hugging her son.

"I don't know Mom. He's a family court judge. I don't know anything about family law."

"Since when has that ever stopped you?"

"But this is different. I've never taken a class on it and the bar didn't cover it. What will I say to him?"

"Be your usual charming self. Tell him you don't know a thing about it, but you will work harder than any clerk he's ever had."

Ben chuckled, "I can't say that."

In the week before the interview, Ben purchased several family law books and read through them as if he was preparing for a family law final exam. When the big day arrived, he felt that he knew as much about the topic as he did any of the other areas he had studied for the bar.

Ben knocked tentatively on Judge Workman's chamber door.

"Come in, come in, young man," welcomed the judge. He was a tall, balding man, with a grey mustache and beard.

Strangely, although Ben had never seen a New Jersey judge, this judge looked exactly like what he had expected. Ben took a chair across from him and sat up very straight.

"So tell me about yourself," said Workman glancing over Ben's resume.

"Well, as you can see, I graduated from Bridgeport School of Law. I think the most fascinating thing about family law is the concept of..."

"I see you worked as a lifeguard," Workman interrupted.

Ben hesitated. "Yes, for several summers. But as I was saying, expanding the penumbra of right to privacy to include..."

"What kind of place was it, a day camp, parks and recreation program?"

Ben smiled. "It started out as a camp for Japanese businessmen's kids, but I ended up running five different swim programs."

"Really?" asked the judge raising his brows. "What kind of a system did you use?"

Ben wrinkled his forehead. He really didn't see what any of this had to do with family law. "I created something called the master stroke system."

Workman brightened. "How very enterprising. I used to be a lifeguard and swim instructor too."

"You were a swim instructor?" Ben asked in surprise.

The judge nodded. "For years and years. My parents often accused me of being part fish. I did more lifeguarding than teaching, but I enjoyed them both. Tell me about your students, what were they like?"

Ben thought back to all the kids he'd taught. Many had come back year after year, each time dramatically improving their skills. "I taught a class of kids with varying skills, even some with disabilities. There was one little boy, Erik, he must have been maybe eight or nine. He had some disease that stunted his muscle growth. He was as light as a feather. I can't remember anymore what the specific disease was called. Truth be told, I don't want to look it up, for fear if I do that I'll learn it's fatal. Anyway, Erik always had the brightest smile. Even though it was difficult for him to move on land, when he got into the water, he was transformed. He became free. It was so cool to watch. He was such a gentle, little thing. It broke my heart to see him struggle the way he did. Yet, he never cried or complained. I'd have to say he was one of my favorite students."

Judge Workman gathered the papers in front of him and stood. "Thank you for coming in Ben, it's been a pleasure."

Ben stood confused. "Don't you want to discuss family law?"

"I talk about that every day. It's not often I get to reminisce about the good old days when I was a lifeguard."

"But how will you know if I have the qualifications you're looking for?"

"I have my ways. Besides I've heard more than enough."

"Oh," Ben sighed hanging his head. It was obvious he wasn't what Workman was looking for.

"In time you'll come to understand family law is more than code and ethics. It's about people, Ben. It's about their past and present, their story. I like your story."

Ben looked up. "Thank you Judge. It was nice meeting you too."

Ben was so impressed with Judge Workman, that he now wanted the job more than he ever had before. It would truly be an honor to work for Judge Workman. As Ben was driving home, he began to worry that he didn't have an opportunity to talk more about family law in the interview. Even though Ben thoroughly enjoyed talking with Judge Workman about lifeguarding, he recognized that there was probably no connection between being a good lifeguard at a swimming pool and a good law clerk in the Family Division of the Superior Court of New Jersey.

As the summer continued, Ben anxiously waited for the mail each day. Then, approximately ten days after the interview, Ben went to his mailbox and saw that he received a letter from the Superior Court of New Jersey. He didn't waste any time and opened the letter while still standing in his driveway. *It was a pleasure to meet with you last week. I would like to take this opportunity to offer the one-year position as my law clerk...* Ben was elated when he read the letter and was so happy that he got the job. He then strolled, smiled and reflected that even though he had been offered many jobs in his lifetime, this was the first time it happened after his accident.

Ben truly enjoyed his time in Judge Workman's court, but as the date for the state bar results grew near, he became quite nervous. His boss had the distinct and unique honor of never having one of his clerks fail the bar. How would Ben break the news to him after getting the results if he didn't pass? Would Workman ask him to resign?

One by one, the twenty-nine other law clerks received their test results in the mail. Ben's stomach wound in knots as he listened to them glee-fully announce passing. What would he do if he was the only one who failed? He didn't think he could show his face in the courthouse again. He hadn't shared the story of his accident or the fact that he had brain damage with any of his fellow clerks. He briefly considered whether to share the story with a few people before his results came back. He knew if he did, the story would quickly spread, giving him an easy excuse if he failed.

"Ben," called a slight receptionist with large green eyes. "You have a phone call. You can pick up on line one."

"Thanks Suzy," he said picking up the phone.

"Ben, I think it's here," gushed an excited Doris. "A large envelope just arrived for you."

"Have you opened it?"

"No sweetheart, I was waiting to see what you wanted me to do."

He took a deep breath. "Open it."

"Are you sure? It can wait until you get home."

"Mom, please don't keep me in suspense."

"Okay, okay."

There was the sound of ripping paper followed by a short silence.

"It says *Congratulations on passing the Bar Exam.*"

"What were my scores on the Multistate Bar Exam?"

Doris paused. "It says 148. Is that good?"

Ben swallowed. "That's in the top percentile of all the test takers! In fact, the score is so high I could actually be a lawyer in some other states without taking their bar exam."

He hung up and stood by the phone in a world of his own, contemplating what he just heard. It was surreal to think that not only did he pass, but he got very high scores.

This news, more so than his neuropsychological tests results or his law school diploma, was a true validation by an independent third party that he was able to again function at a very high level. Although he was not pleased to learn some of his friends hadn't passed, knowing that high functioning, intelligent people had failed, reinforced his confidence that he had overcome the impossible.

Despite his severe brain damage, he passed the New Jersey, Pennsylvania and Multistate Bar exams on the first taking. The neuropsychologist, Dawn, his brother, and his parents had told him his potential was limitless, but until that moment, he had never truly believed it. Now he knew. There was no stopping him. He would always be able to do anything he ever wanted to, as long as he was willing to put in the effort.

A week later, Ben's family gathered at the courthouse to watch Ben be sworn in as a licensed attorney in the State of New Jersey. He could have gone to a general ceremony in Trenton, New Jersey, to be sworn in as an attorney, but he wanted something extra special.

"Ben has come before us today to take the oath to uphold the New Jersey and United States Constitution," Judge Workman addressed the gathering. "Not only is he one of the hardest working law clerks I've ever worked with, he has overcome odds beyond most of our comprehension."

Doris dabbed at her eyes. "To think that four years ago there wasn't a doctor in in any of the hospitals who ever envisioned that this day would ever come."

"I did," said Hank.

"How can you say that?"

"Shhh, they're starting," he whispered giving her a wink.

"Raise your right hand and repeat after me," said Judge Workman.

Ben held up his hand.

"I promise to uphold and protect the Constitution of the United States and the Constitution of the State of New Jersey..."

Ben smiled as he repeated the words he waited so long to say.

The image of the photographs of him in a coma on full life support flashed through his head.

He thought about all he'd sacrificed to make it to this point, and felt confident that after what he'd been through, there was nothing he couldn't endure.

Ben turned to look at his family and a lump rose in his throat as he spoke the last words. He could never have come this far without their love and support.

"By the power vested in me by the great state of New Jersey, please welcome our newest officially licensed attorney!"

Ben's family surrounded him, while hugging and kissing him. For one brief second, life went into slow motion as he truly savored just being in the moment. He wished it was possible to bottle time, because he didn't think he could be happier.

* * *

From that day forward, Ben always lived life upholding two principles. The first was his oath as an attorney. The second was a combination of Coach Mainieri's rule and what his accident had taught him, to stay in the moment and when times became too tough to handle, to get through it by trying twice as hard for as long as possible. I know with certainty that these two life principles work, because the story that you have just read, the most significant case of my entire career, is actually the story of me, when I attended the College of New Jersey. This is my story. I am Ben!

204

Chapter Thirty-Six

FULL CIRCLE

You could hear a pin drop in the gym when I revealed that the story I just told was my own. The kids who had previously been lounging against the bleachers, were now sitting forward in disbelief. After a few moments of silence, the audience would cheer while giving me a standing ovation.

"For years I have wondered how one drunk driver could have done so much harm to my family and me. While I was in the hospital, I promised myself that if I was fortunate enough to fulfill my dream of having a full recovery, in spite of all of the doctors saying it was not possible, that I would spend the rest of my life doing two things. I promised that I would do everything that I could to end drunk driving, because a drunk driver did this to me. I also promised myself that I would spend the rest of my life helping the brain and catastrophically injured, by providing them with needed hope and inspiration."

I paced the length of the room as all eyes followed me. I didn't want the audience to misunderstand what I was about to say to mean that I in any way condoned their drinking alcohol. Yet, I realized that there still might be some students in the audience who were going to drink, regardless of what I might say.

"I have two very important messages. First, if you're going to make the decision to drink, never make the next decision to drive. Making that decision can impact and horribly change your life and the lives of so many people. In my case, the driver was able to walk away. He didn't have to deal with the long-term consequences of his actions that I had to. But I'd like to remind you that you may not be so lucky. If you drink and drive, it may be you that ends up in my position or worse. You may kill your mother, your sibling, or your best friend. I don't know about you, but I wouldn't want to be the one to live with that guilt for the rest of my life. I am asking everyone in this auditorium to make the decision right now that you will never drive after having even one drink. Give the keys to a friend beforehand, call a cab, or call your family."

"Yeah right," called my heckler from earlier. "No one in his right mind is gonna call their parents. It would be suicide."

A low murmur broke out over my audience, as many students agreed.

"I know, I know, it sounds like a crazy plan. But every parent out there would much prefer to get a call from you after drinking, than getting a call from a police officer or a county morgue."

"And then grounding my ass when I get home!"

"Let me add that every one of you in this audience now has a lawyer. His name is Steven Benvenisti. I've made and obtained Trademark rights to a contract for each and every one of you. It's called the *Contract for Life*. It's an agreement between you and one or both of your parents. It essentially states that if your parent gets that phone call from you for a ride home — that your parent promises to come get you and drive you and your friends home. Your parent further promises that no punishment will follow because of that phone call. In fact, you will be congratulated for making the responsible decision. I've been told on many occasions that the contract has worked and both sides have kept their promises."

Skeptical whispers rose from the crowd as students thought about what I'd just said.

My voice rose over them, "The second message I have, is that you will have many experiences in your lives when your friends make the decision to drink. If that friend tries to drive, not only is it very important that you don't get in the car with him or her, you need to do everything in your power to stop that person from driving. They may be angry with you that night, but he or she will be alive to come up to you the next day and thank you for saving their life.

"Everyone knows that reflexes, judgment and coordination are all temporarily impaired after drinking. What breaks my heart to this day is that with each horrible DWI accident, there are so many simple things which could have been done differently to prevent the tragedy.

"All it takes is one person who volunteers to be the designated driver. That person doesn't drink and promises to bring everyone home. Or they can make sure everyone stays the night where they are. Or they can call a taxi for you. Any questions?"

Several hands shot up in the air. I pointed to a girl in the first row. "Yes?"

"What happened to the drunk driver that hit you?"

"Unfortunately, not very much. Since my accident wasn't a fatality, the criminal laws in Florida at the time didn't offer a lot of protection for severely injured parties. My case never went to court. The drunk driver did a few days in jail and that was it. I didn't even have a civil case against him, because he had no insurance and had nothing I could collect from him. We tried to go after the bar that he drank and worked at, but it too had no insurance."

"Then how were your medical bills covered?"

"Fortunately, New Jersey had a no-fault law that covered all my medical bills, regardless of the amount. Just months after my accident, the law changed and created a cap of $250,000 in medical bill payments for all car related accidents. That would have covered a fraction of my overall care. I'm convinced that if I had my accident just a few months later when the law changed, that my recovery would not have turned out the way it did."

"Why don't you talk more about all that in your story? Why don't you say what happened to the drunk driver?"

"Because this is my story. I want people to understand what happens to the victims and survivors. I'm less concerned about the drunk driver who hit me. I'm not angry with him, but I don't forgive him either. He's taken enough time up in my life. He doesn't deserve a second more of my attention."

"What about running? Do you still do that?"

"Two to three miles every day, at a speed of 7.8 mph," I smiled and pressed a button on my PowerPoint remote. Instantly, a video appeared on the screen of me sprinting on a treadmill.

"What happened to Dawn?" asked another student. "Are you still with her?"

"Yes. We've been married for more than a decade and have two children."

My enthusiastic audience dispensed with hand raising and shouting of questions as if we were at a press conference.

"What kind of lawyer are you?"

"I'm a personal injury attorney."

The audience laughed at the appropriateness of my answer.

"For some reason, the public has been conditioned to think that after an accident, insurance companies throw large sums of money to accident victims. In reality, in virtually every single case throughout the country, attorneys have to fight very hard to obtain each and every dollar for their clients. Virtually every claim is fought aggressively by the insurance companies. Insurance companies have powerful lawyers, with medical doctors on their team, aggressively attempting to defer fault away from them and then minimize each and every injury claimed. Unfortunately, the public doesn't hear about the enormous uphill battle every single accident victim faces in attempting to get their lives back together.

Curtis suddenly called out of turn, "You went through all that and still ended up like every other adult. Why should we worry then?"

Curtis may have thought his words would stump me, but it didn't work. I didn't tell my story in hopes of scaring students. After all, most kids like the mouthy Curtis have an, "It will never happen to me" attitude. Instead, I left my audience with a different thought.

"As a personal injury attorney, I often never get to meet my D.W.I. victim clients, because they have already died in these completely preventable accidents. Most of the estates I represent are of young students innocently killed by drunk drivers. Although I never met these deceased individuals, I meet each and every one of their killers. I meet them in a proceeding called a deposition, which usually takes place more than a year after the accident in a prison. I get to ask the drunk drivers questions, under oath, about their lives and the circumstances that led up to the tragedy.

"They always tell me the worst part of the drinking and driving experience, even more terrifying than spending years locked up with people who've committed heinous crimes, is falling asleep at night. When they try to fall asleep, they start to think about what they did. They realize that someone's little girl or boy, someone's best friend or brother, someone's parent or grandparent, is dead and buried because of a stupid, meaningless, mistake they made. Their shame is tremendous. They know, no matter what they do or where they go, they will never have another peaceful night's sleep as long as they live.

"So, the next time you're looking at those keys after even having even one drink of alcohol, ask yourself, 'Do I want this drink to be the drink that virtually guarantees that for 365 nights a year, for the rest of my life, I won't be able to sleep comfortably, because I'm overwhelmed and consumed with guilt for one mistake I made on one night of my life?'

"So, in closing, I'd like to ask each and every person sitting in this auditorium to make a promise to yourself right now. Promise yourself that no matter where you are, or how close you are to your next destination, the next time you make a decision to drink alcohol, that you will never then make the decision to operate a vehicle. By keeping this promise that you made today, you may very well have guaranteed a much longer and happier life for yourself, your friends, loved ones, and even a complete stranger who will never know that the decision you made today just gave them many more years of life and happiness."

THE SECRET TO SUCCESS

Your emotions are controlled by what it is that you're thinking about

~ Steven Benvenisti, 1989

As much as I appreciate being told that I have come very far and accomplished much more than anyone could imagine since my accident at age twenty-one, I believe my current success has little to do with my medical recovery. Success should never be defined by one's actual accomplishments in life. Neither should success be measured by one's actual life circumstances, no matter how wonderful they may appear to be. Rather, I've always believed that a person has achieved the highest level of success when they have found "happiness." Unfortunately, most do not include "happiness" in their definition of success and even if they do, they have no idea how to achieve it.

Most people believe that success is achieved when one has attained "wealth." Yet the wealthiest among us are usually not the happiest. Movie and music stars who have all the money and wealth anyone could ever want, are the same groups of people who have a higher prevalence of depression, drug use, and even suicide.

Others believe that success is achieved when one has attained "good health." Yet, many people who are healthy take their good health for granted and are never truly happy. Or they could be healthy, but still consume themselves with complaining and negativity.

After awakening from the coma and starting to realize everything that had been taken away from me because of the accident, the goal of "happiness" was so unbelievably far-fetched and unrealistic. I was living with the consequences of severe brain damage, was in continuous excruciating pain, couldn't think straight, couldn't move my legs or care for myself, and was told that there would be little, if any, improvement. My physical and cognitive problems put me at the lowest emotional level a human being could be at and I had no idea how I could ever come close to being happy again.

The turning point in my emotional recovery was when I realized that my pre-accident happiness had nothing to do with my good health, my grade point average, or even my social life. The only reason why I was happy before the accident was because I chose to consume my mind with thoughts that put a smile on my face. In fact, the only reason why anyone is happy or unhappy at any given time has little to do with their actual circumstances in life and has everything to do with what they are thinking about.

I've been asked, 'How could what I think about have an impact on my feelings?' My response is to picture someone with a five day per week, thirty minute commute to work. During that commute to work, that person could be thinking, 'I hate my job' or 'I don't make enough money' or 'I'll never be able to retire on this income' or 'I hate my boss.' **While** thinking those negative thoughts, that person is guaranteed to be unhappy. Thinking those thoughts for the entire thirty minute commute will guarantee an unhappy commute to work. If that same person is in the habit of thinking unpleasant thoughts, then he or she will most certainly be an unhappy person.

Now picture that same person commuting to work, except now is thinking happier thoughts such as, 'I am so fortunate to be employed in this difficult economy' or 'I'm looking forward to seeing Joe or Jackie when I get to work' or 'it's so nice to be needed at work' or even 'one day I'm going to win the lottery.' It really doesn't matter whether the thoughts are realistic or not, as long as they are pleasant. **While** thinking those pleasant thoughts, that person is guaranteed to be happy. If that same person is in the habit of thinking pleasant thoughts, then he or she will most certainly be a happy person. This concept is different from thinking positively, though thinking positively automatically follows. Rather, it simply involves consuming your mind with thoughts that put a smile on your face. It doesn't matter what your actual circumstances are. It doesn't even matter if what you're thinking about is realistic. It simply requires consuming your free time thinking about thoughts which are pleasant, and not ones that are unpleasant.

While hospitalized, as soon as I realized that being happy in the present moment simply involved changing what I decided to think about, everything changed. I also realized that most of my grief came from comparing myself with who I was before the accident and the fun life I was missing out on.

I realized that I needed to change what it was that I was thinking about, or my depression would get out of control. It wasn't easy, but instead of thinking about all the great times I was missing with my college friends, I thought about how nice it was to be with my family, to have a girlfriend I could talk to, to watch TV, and eat whenever I wanted to. When I was in cognitive therapy, instead of thinking about how sad it was that I was no longer an active college student earning credits toward graduation, I thought about how cool it was that the more I read, the easier it was to understand what it was that I was reading. Instead of thinking about how sad it was that I could no longer be the same athlete who won the one-mile race before the accident, I made my new sense of athletic purpose trying to walk a little further on the parallel bars without falling into my therapist's arms. Every time sad thoughts about the past, present or future would creep into my mind, I would force myself to think about things which would put a smile on my face. As the months of my hospitalization continued, I gradually came out of my depression. That way of thinking continued through my three years of law school and the decades that followed as an attorney through today.

I genuinely believe that the definition of success is finding happiness and getting there simply involves making sure that you are consistently thinking thoughts which put a smile on your face. I am absolutely convinced that anyone can find happiness if they're willing to get into the habit of consistently changing what they decide to think about and making sure that those thoughts are pleasant ones. To put it simply: Your emotions are controlled by what it is that you're thinking about.

ADVICE FOR SPECIAL GROUPS

ATTORNEYS

While I was in a coma, my father first began looking for a personal injury attorney to handle any civil action which may follow because of my accident. Being from New Jersey and not knowing any Florida attorneys, he didn't have a clue as to who was the best, or who to trust. So he went through the yellow pages and started making calls. Most attorneys smelled money and were quite eager to take the case. They got right down to business asking specifics and proposing their strategy.

But when my father called one attorney, whose name was Eilon, he got a very different response. The first thing Eilon asked him was, "How are you holding up?" The second thing he asked was, "How are your wife and son doing?" My father appreciated that he appeared to genuinely care about issues other than the potential for financial recovery or what was in it for him. Based on these very unscientific criteria, Eilon was chosen as the attorney to handle any case which may have followed my serious accident.

Eilon was a man who understood that clients are people going through difficult times, and not just pay checks. He became our friend and ally in a fight we neither understood nor had the energy to participate in. Even though the lawsuit went on for years, and the results were uncollectible judgments against the drunk driver and bar at which he drank at, we never regretted the decision to hire Eilon.

When I became an attorney, I always remembered to treat potential clients the way Eilon treated my father during that first phone call. Remember, no matter how strong the urge to get down to case specifics, always make sure to treat potential clients as people who've just been through a traumatic event. It just might turn out to be the most significant case of your entire career.

NURSES AND REHABILITATION PROFESSIONALS

I couldn't have accomplished what I did in my recovery without the nurses and rehabilitation professionals who taught me, step by step, how to do virtually everything all over again. Before and after my daily grueling rehabilitation, the nurses encouraged me and pushed me to keep going and not give up. For that reason and many others, I, as well as many patients and their families that I've spoken with, hold nurses and rehabilitation professionals in the highest regard.

I've found that nurses and rehabilitation professionals that are able to show warmth and compassion are dramatically more effective than those who do not. It is these nurses and rehabilitation professionals who patients and families put on a pedestal. In fact, most patients assume that the nurses and rehab professionals are the ones who are most familiar with their medical condition. Even though it may not be accurate, patients and families assume that the nurses and rehab professionals are extremely familiar with their entire medical chart and review it with their doctors regularly.

What some doctors' lack, and nurses and rehabilitation professionals have, is the ability to fully realize a patient and family's emotional concerns. Compassionate nurses and rehabilitation professionals realize that when a patient or family member begins a dialog about their concerns, they're not always expecting an answer. Most of the time, the patient or family member simply wants to express what they're going through and come "full circle" with whatever they're voicing. Once the patient or family member fully expresses what they want to communicate, they often feel their concern has been dealt with by the medical professional who is listening. Therefore, know that when you take the time to listen, you are doing more to aid in the healing process than you could ever imagine.

FAMILIES OF VICTIMS AND SURVIVORS

Even after having gone through what I went through and after representing thousands of individuals and families in my career, it wasn't until I had children that I realized that I am still no closer to truly understanding what my accident experience must have been like for my parents and family. I often wonder who has it worse, the victim who experiences the physical trauma and aftermath, or the family and loved ones who have to watch it happen. Every parent, family member and loved one of a traumatically injured individual go through enormous pain and suffering, which can't be measured.

I've learned that when one experiences overwhelming stress, whether because of dealing with a loved one post-injury, or simply dealing with the struggles that life has to offer, that it is best to be guided by two general principles.

The first is to always take life one moment at a time. Whatever you do, stay in the present and don't try to think about and take on challenges that aren't before you now, and quite frankly, may never be before you. Although it is common to find oneself unnecessarily worrying about the future, the key to making it through life's stressful situations is to stay focused on the present. All that is real is right now.

The second is to maintain a sense of balance. This won't come naturally for most individuals, especially when dealing with stressful situations. Maintaining balance means to set aside time to do enjoyable activities. Whether it is to watch TV, read a book, go for a walk, or to be intimate with your significant other, it is essential to do anything

positive that removes you from your present environment of respon-
sibilities and stress. When it comes to parents, family members, or
caregivers, that means don't devote every spare minute and emotion to
caring for your loved one. Time needs to be set aside for other activities. Though it may be difficult to keep guilt from creeping in while
you're doing enjoyable activities to maintain balance, think of it like the
instructions flight attendants give passengers before take-off. In case
of emergency, they instruct parents to put the oxygen mask over their
own face before securing one on their children. In the same way, family members, loved ones and caregivers of trauma patients, must give
themselves a chance to rejuvenate in order to be helpful to their loved
one. Failing to maintain a sense of balance in one's routine will result
in a gradual decline in mood, energy level, and health. Ultimately, total
burnout could develop.

IN APPRECIATION

A very special thank you to my parents, without whose love and support I would never have survived.

Thanks also to my siblings Debbie, Michelle, and especially Bruce, who risked his career to be by my side throughout the hospitalization and recovery.

My appreciation is further expressed to all families who have supported loved ones after the devastation of a D.W.I. crash. Though your loved one may not be able to express it, your support and sacrifices mean the world.

I would like to further express my appreciation for the many who work with Mothers Against Drunk Driving (M.A.D.D.). You were there for my family and me to support us during a time when society didn't fully appreciate the horrific consequences of D.W.I. So many of the people who work with M.A.D.D. have lost so much due to a drunk driver, yet you so selflessly find the strength and conviction to devote your lives to supporting such a wonderful organization. It is my honor and privilege to work with you.

I would also like to thank all the organizations with their mission devoted to improve the lives of those dealing with brain injury. You so effectively work to help the public understand the "silent epidemic" of our time that impacts the lives of so many, including our brave troops returning from combat.

I would like to also recognize the medical professionals who brought me back from the brink of death, the nurses who cared for me and made life bearable, and the therapists who gave me the confidence and courage to walk, talk, read, and truly live again. I offer my heartfelt gratitude for all you did for me and all you have done and continue to do for your patients. Additionally, patients would not have the benefit of the aforesaid medical professionals without the heroic and lifesaving efforts of the police and emergency medical personnel who so courageously save lives every single day.

Finally, I would like to thank my law firm's partners Samuel L. Davis, Marc C. Saperstein, Garry R. Salomon, and Paul Garfield, along with the attorneys and staff, who share my strong conviction against driving while intoxicated and who have devoted their careers to advocating for our clients who have lost so much.

CONTACT INFORMATION

To contact Steven Benvenisti visit: www.springbreakbook.com

CONTRACT FOR LIFE

THIS AGREEMENT IS A LEGALLY BINDING CONTRACT made on this _____ day of _____ in the year 20_____ by and between the undersigned individual, hereinafter referred to as the "TEENAGER;" and the other Individual(s) hereinafter referred to as the PARENT(S);

WHEREAS, the TEENAGER is a normal, healthy teen who unfortunately, will from time to time, do things he or she should not be doing, such as drinking alcohol with other teenagers; and

WHEREAS, the PARENT(S) do not accept this type of behavior and strongly forbid the TEENAGER from engaging in underage drinking and/or the use of illegal drugs; and

WHEREAS, this Agreement shall not be construed to constitute acceptance or permission for the TEENAGER to engage in such behavior; nor shall it be construed to give express or implied permission by the PARENT(S) to engage in such activity; and

WHEREAS, the PARENT(S) love and cherish their child and desire to see no harm come to them, no matter what the circumstances;

WITNESSETH:

NOW THEREFORE, in consideration of the love between the PARENT(S) and the TEENAGER, it is agreed as follows:

1. In the event that the TEENAGER drinks alcohol, it is agreed that the TEENAGER will not operate a motor vehicle and will not get a ride from anyone who has consumed alcohol; and hereby further promises to call his or her PARENT(S) for a "No Questions Asked" free ride home for the TEENAGER and his or her friends.

2. The PARENT(S) agree to pick up the TEENAGER and their FRIENDS without any "hassle" and shall not ask at that time any questions of them or of their friends regarding their behavior that evening.

3. PARENT(S) agree not to punish the TEENAGER for drinking; but rather recognize their good judgment for conducting themselves responsibly by calling PARENT(S) for a safe ride home.

4. TEENAGER agrees to wear his or her seatbelt while in a car and shall require all passengers within his or her car to wear a seatbelt.

In Witness Whereof the parties hereto have affixed their signatures below

_____   _____
TEENAGER   PARENT(S)

Prepared by:
Steven Benvenisti, Esq. • Davis, Saperstein & Salomon, P.C. • www.stopdwinow.org • steven@dsslaw.com
1-800-529-2000
© 2007 Contract for Life. Copyright restrictions on us, by Parents and Teens are hereby waived.

Contract For Life **which forms the binding agreement between the student and parent(s) to never drive after having even one drink of alcohol.**